ISEB Certificate in Requirements Engineering*

Self Study
Just Enough Essential Points ('JEEP') Manual

©Guy Beauchamp 2009

Please be aware that it is illegal to copy and/or otherwise distribute all or part of this copyrighted manual.

FIRST EDITION

ISBN 978-1-4092-5971-8

*Note: this manual is not endorsed or sanctioned in any way by BCS or ISEB.

Questions? ISEBRE@smart-BA.com

ISEB Certificate in Requirements Engineering
Self Study 'JEEP' Manual

CONTENTS

Introduction:..3
What ISEB expects of Requirements Engineers 5
Requirements Engineering Syllabus Sections..5
ISEB Syllabus Section 1: Lifecycle for business change 6
ISEB Syllabus Section 2: Nature and problems of Requirements 10
ISEB Syllabus Section 2 exam style revision question..15
ISEB Syllabus Section 2 exam style revision question MODEL ANSWER 16
ISEB Syllabus Section 3 Hierarchy of Requirements 18
ISEB Syllabus Section 3 exam style revision question..26
ISEB Syllabus Section 3 exam style revision question MODEL ANSWER 27
ISEB Syllabus Section 4: Stakeholders in the Requirement Process 28
ISEB Syllabus Section 4 exam style revision question..31
ISEB Syllabus Section 4 exam style revision question MODEL ANSWER 33
ISEB Syllabus Section 5: Requirements Elicitation...34
ISEB Syllabus Section 5 exam style revision question..42
ISEB Syllabus Section 5 exam style revision question MODEL ANSWER 43
ISEB Syllabus Section 6: Use of Models in Requirements Engineering 44
ISEB Syllabus Section 6 exam style revision question – process model 58
ISEB Syllabus Section 6 exam style revision question – data model 59
ISEB Syllabus Section 6 exam style revision question – process model MODEL ANSWER 60
ISEB Syllabus Section 6 exam style revision question – data model MODEL ANSWER....................61
ISEB Syllabus Section 7: Documenting the Requirements...62
ISEB Syllabus Section 7 exam style revision question..67
ISEB Syllabus Section 7 exam style revision question MODEL ANSWER 68
ISEB Syllabus Section 8: Requirements Analysis 69
ISEB Syllabus Section 8 exam style revision question..74
ISEB Syllabus Section 8 exam style revision question MODEL ANSWER 75
ISEB Syllabus Section 9: Requirements Validation 76
ISEB Syllabus Section 9 exam style revision question..85
ISEB Syllabus Section 9 exam style revision question MODEL ANSWER 86
ISEB Syllabus Section 10: Requirements Management 90
ISEB Syllabus Section 10 exam style revision question..97
ISEB Syllabus Section 10 exam style revision question MODEL ANSWER 98
ISEB Syllabus Section 11: Benefits Confirmation...99
ISEB Syllabus Section 11 exam style revision question..104
ISEB Syllabus Section 11 exam style revision question MODEL ANSWER 105
Maximise your marks in the ISEB Requirements Engineering exam 106
ISEB Requirements Engineering Sample Exam Paper and Marking Scheme 108
MOCK EXAM PAPER – SBA/RE/001/v1.0 109
Review of ISEB Requirements Engineering Objectives..116
Glossary of terms 117

Questions? ISEBRE@smart-BA.com

ISEB Certificate in Requirements Engineering
Self Study 'JEEP' Manual

Introduction:

Hello and welcome to the smart-BA distance learning programme for the ISEB Diploma in Business Analysis. In this manual you will learn just what you need to learn in order to prepare for the ISEB Certificate in Requirements Engineering – one of the four certificates you need to pass in order to achieve the Diploma. This is a JEEP manual: Just Enough Essential Points to help you pass the exam.

Who is the manual for?
- Business Analysts who know the subject area and don't need a classroom based course
- Business Analysts who already know the fundamentals of what business analysis is all about
- Business Analysts who have already captured requirements, modelled business processes and perhaps even modelled data requirements on a change project involving computerised solutions
- Business Analysts who have familiarity with the principle concepts of computers

Who is the manual NOT for?
- those who have no experience of Business Analysis
- those who do not know what a requirement is or what a process model looks like
- those who have not already worked as a Business Analyst on change projects
- those with no familiarity of analysing requirements for computerised solutions

Key points:
- Requirements Engineering certificate focus is on defining and managing requirements
- This manual focuses solely on the ISEB Certificate in Requirements Engineering
- The manual format is to present each section of the ISEB Syllabus in order and each section will contain
  - Information you need to know about the ISEB Syllabus section
  - Suggestions for further reading
  - Exam style revision question
  - Mock exam when you have completed the manual
- This is a self study manual – but if you need help contact ISEBRE@smart-BA.com
- **Please be aware that it is illegal to copy and/or otherwise distribute all or part of this copyrighted manual.**

Detail:
This manual is concerned with the ISEB Certificate in Requirements Engineering approach to requirements definition and management. Its focus is on using a systematic approach to eliciting, analysing, validating, documenting and managing requirements.

Although the manual focus is on covering the material you need to cover in order to pass the exam, a lot of what you will learn will be useful to you as a Business Analyst as well. Bear in mind though that the ISEB Diploma in Business Analysis is focused on Business Analysis of new IT systems and will primarily be about analysis of those systems, whereas you may find as a Business Analyst that you also have to specify requirements for non-IT components of solutions.

©Guy Beauchamp 2009
Questions? ISEBRE@smart-BA.com

Because the manual is geared towards passing the exam the format has been designed to cover each section of the syllabus in turn. There is suggested further reading for each sections and for most but not all sections you can test your understanding with a question in the style of an actual exam – there is a model answer and you can also have your answer marked by an accredited ISEB exam marker.

Having completed the syllabus in this fashion, there is a mock exam for you to take on your own – again a model answer is presented and you can also have your answers marked by an accredited ISEB exam marker. It goes without saying that you should approach the exam questions and mock exams with complete honesty: the objective is to find any weaknesses in your understanding BEFORE the exam so cheating at this stage will only degrade your chances of passing the exam.

This is a self study manual but should you need to discuss or clarify anything please do not hesitate to contact ISEBRE@smart-BA.com

What ISEB expects of Requirements Engineers

Holders of the ISEB Certificate in Requirements Engineering should be able to
- Describe the roles and responsibilities of key stakeholders in the requirements engineering process
- Demonstrate the application of a range of requirements elicitation techniques
- Explain the use of requirements elicitation techniques and the relevance of the techniques to given situations
- Document and prioritise user requirements for an information system
- Identify problems with requirements and explain how requirements documentation may be improved
- Create a process/function model of requirements for an information system
- Interpret a model of the data requirements for an information system
- Explain the importance of linking project objectives and requirements to the Business Case
- Describe the principles of Requirements Management and explain the importance of managing requirements
- Describe the use of CASE tools to support Requirements Engineering
- Explain the principles of Requirements Validation and define an approach to validating requirements

This is from the BCS ISEB web page http://www.bcs.org/server.php?show=nav.7738. Read these objectives now and when you have completed the manual and check that can satisfy them.

Requirements Engineering Syllabus Sections

1. Lifecycle for business change
2. Nature and problems of Requirements
3. Hierarchy of Requirements
4. Stakeholders in the Requirements process
5. Requirements Elicitation
6. Use of models in requirements engineering
7. Documenting the requirements
8. Requirements Analysis
9. Requirements Validation
10. Requirements Management
11. Benefits Confirmation

These are the elements of the syllabus set by ISEB. The following sections are presented in that order.

ISEB Syllabus Section 1: Lifecycle for business change

Key Points:

There is no standard definition of these phases but generically they are

Identify change required for whatever reasons

Analyse requirements for what the organisation needs to be able to do in order to make the change

Specify solution that implements the requirements

Develop solution that has been specified

Test solution delivers the requirements

Rollout solution to the end users

Monitor solution success in achieving the change objectives

Questions? ISEBRE@smart-BA.com

smart·BA
distance learning programme

Detail:

Identify change required for whatever reasons such as

- Strategy the organisation needs to adopt (strategic projects)
- Legal and regulatory compliance projects that are required in order to keep the business trading under the laws and rules it needs to obey
- Tactical response to a problem that confronts the organisation (tactical projects and enhancements).
- Tactical response to an opportunity that the organisation identifies (tactical projects and enhancements)
- On-going quality improvement programme (enhancements)
- Organisational change (from internal team reorganisation up to merges and acquisitions)
- Etc – there can be other reasons for change: this is not an exhaustive list

Analyse requirements for what the organisation needs to be able to do in order to make the change
How will the business know that it has achieved the changes it wants to make? The answer is that it has achieved certain objectives that measure how much the business has changed. Once it hits a certain target for an objectives, it declares that objective as achieved. A typical project will have half a dozen objectives.

What needs to change in order that the target for each objective can be achieved? The answer is the requirements define what needs to change without specifying how (that is the solution and will be designed once the objectives and requirements have been defined and agreed by all who need to).

Specify solution that implements the requirements
In terms of ISEB the solution will involve a computerised solution, but it does not have to. In any event, the solution will always involve changes that the business needs to make as well as any computerised solution. Computer applications do not run in a vacuum: users at locations running certain business processes will use the applications in order to achieve business objectives.
The solution that gets specified will need to specify all the components computerised or not in order to make sure that the whole solution works end to end.
In order to be able to do that the solutions specified will need to know all the requirements that a solution will be defined for.

Develop solution that has been specified
The computerised components will need coding, organisational changes will need preparation, negotiation and communication, location changes will need planning and co-ordinating, procedure changes will need developing and so on.

Test solution delivers the requirements
Testing is large subject area in its own right. The details of how to construct full test plans are out scope for this manual. What is pertinent is that the when the solution is ready for user acceptance testing (UAT), the test that are run perform agreed tests that prove to user satisfaction that that requirements have been built in to the solution.

Rollout solution to the end users

Questions? ISEBRE@smart-BA.com

There are many ways to implement change (pilots, phased rollout, big-bang implementation and so on), and in the period of transitioning from the old to the new there will be an interim period where change management will be required. The rollout strategy to be adopted and design of cutover activities are out of scope for this manual.

Monitor solution success in achieving the change objectives
In order to be able to declare the project a success it must be possible to prove that it has achieved its objectives. Therefore those objectives and targets must have been defined, the requirements for the changes required to achieve the objectives must have been analysed and there must be a method for reporting on that achievement.

Remember: although the focus in the ISEB Certificate in Requirements Engineering is on requirements for computerised components of a solution, there is no logical reason why the above lifecycle would not work for non-computerised components as well.

Questions? ISEBRE@smart-BA.com

Further Reading for Syllabus Section 1

Business Analysis – Debra Paul and Donald Yeates
Published by: The British Computer Society
ISBN 1-902505-70-0
Price: £20.00 from BCS and Amazon etc
Relevant Chapters/sections:
Chapter 9 – Requirements Engineering
       section The Place of Requirements Engineering in the SDLC pages137-139

Requirements Engineering by Gerald Kotonya and Ian Sommerville
Published by: John Willey & Sons
ISBN: 0-471-97208-8
Price: £36.00 from Amazon etc
Relevant Chapters/sections:
Chapter 1 – Introduction

Questions? ISEBRE@smart-BA.com

ISEB Syllabus Section 2: Nature and problems of Requirements

Key points:

A requirement is a defined change required in order to achieve project objectives.

Problems of requirements
- Poor specification due to
    o Ambiguity
    o poor definition of terms
    o conflicting requirements
    o solution not requirement
- Out of scope requirements
- Requirements that do not satisfy the definition of what a requirement is!

Detail:

IEEE definition of a requirement
1. a condition or capability needed by a user to solve a problem or achieve an objective
2. a condition or capability that must be met or possessed by a system or system component to satisfy a contract, standard, specification, or other formally imposed document
3. a documented representation of a condition or capability as in (1) or (2)

The main problems with requirements are due to a lack of rigour which is in turn due to the fact they are defined in English and ambiguity is inherent in English as we will see.
The other major reasons for problems with requirements are
- Failure to validate they are required to achieve objectives – in other words they are by definition out of scope
- Poor categorisation of requirements – that is an element that has been declared to be a requirement but does not fit the definition of a requirement.

The next couple of pages will look at these problems in more detail.

Problems with requirements I – Poor specification due to:

Ambiguity

Ambiguous requirements are requirements where elements of that requirement can be interpreted in more than one way and there is no indication about which is the right way to interpret it.

Example an ambiguous requirement: "A diary system is needed". Is "diary" a history of events or a planned schedule of actions or both or something else altogether?

Poor definition of terms

A "term" is word or phrase in a requirement. If a term has not been defined either in the requirement or as part of a glossary of terms, the requirement ambiguous. Worse still, users and business analysts can assume they know what the term means, but each can make a different assumption about the meaning.

Example: in the requirement "the system should monitor sales activity" what does "monitor" mean? Does it mean run reports on sales, or does it mean that when sales hit a certain level something happens (what?)? Does it mean something else?

Conflicting requirements

Given that requirements at a low level can run in to hundreds, it is not difficult for requirements documented at different times and perhaps generated by different users and documented by different analysts to conflict with each other,

Example: "The system should allocate orders to sales staff" and "The system should allow sales staff to pick an order to work on" may be in conflict with each other.

Solution not requirement

It is very easy to anticipate how a solution COULD work and incorporate this in to the requirements. The problem is this may not be the best way for the solution to work and the actual requirement has not been fully captured.

Example: "Sales staff must be able to email the customer" – does it have to be email? If not, then using the word "email" limits how the solution can be designed with no justification for limiting it in this way – and there may be better solutions than email. Take the solution email out the requirement such as "Sales staff must be able to send messages to the customer" and the solutions designers can propose other solutions such as letter, SMS, couriers, or whatever helps achieve the objectives best.

Problems with requirements II – Out of scope requirements

Remember: a requirement is a defined change required in order to achieve project objectives. Objectives define what needs to be achieved in order for a project to be considered successful and requirements define what needs to change in order to achieve the objectives. Objectives are measures that can increased, decreased or maintained and if they hit a certain target value equate to project success.

A requirement is out of scope if it does not contribute to achieving objectives.

Example: Suppose a project's objective is to decrease the cost of recording a sale.
Is the requirement "the system should allow users to record suppliers name and address" contributing to achieving that objective?

There is a 2 way link between requirements and objectives.

Every objective must have at least one requirement which – if implemented in the solution – will yield that objective. Normally, a project will have many objectives (up to around 10) and there are many requirements for each objective.

Each requirement will contribute to achieving at least one objective. Normally, a requirement will contribute to more than one objective. If you find that you have a compelling requirement which has no objectives it contributes to one of 2 conclusions can be drawn:
1. The requirement is out of scope because it does not contribute to achieving any project objectives
2. The project has failed to identify one of it's objectives – and this is very serious as if it is missing one of it's objectives it also missing the other requirements that contribute to achieving that missing objective.

Problems with requirements III – Requirements that do not satisfy the definition of what a requirement is.

Remember: a requirement is a defined change required in order to achieve project objectives.

Consider the following example 'requirement': "The project will take no longer than 3 months." This is not a requirement (as defined above) – it is a constraint on the project. N.B.: you will do further work on problems with requirements during ISEB Section 8 Requirements Analysis.

All too often 'requirements' are generated that are not really requirements at all – although it may be another component in the analysis (as in the example above). A very common mistake is to categorise an objective as a requirement and vice-versa.

Example: "reduce the cost of taking orders" is an objective, not a requirement, and "be able to identify premium customers" is a requirement and not an objective.

Remember: Objectives are measures that can increased, decreased or maintained and if they hit a certain target value equate to project success.
Requirements are changes required in order to achieve project objectives.

Questions? ISEBRE@smart-BA.com

Further Reading for Syllabus Section 2

Business Analysis – Debra Paul and Donald Yeates
Published by: The British Computer Society
ISBN 1-902505-70-0
Price: £20.00 from BCS and Amazon etc
Relevant Chapters/sections:
Chapter 9 – Requirements Engineering
> section The Problems With Requirements pages135-137 and
> section Requirements Analysis
> pages 147-149

Questions? ISEBRE@smart-BA.com

ISEB Syllabus Section 2 exam style revision question

Ultimate Catalogue Company has initiated a project which has an objective to reduce the percentage of orders returned due incorrect delivery address by 66%.

Review the following requirements identifying any errors or areas for improvement. If appropriate suggest what changes should be made.

Requirement	Your review
The system should be easier to use than the current system.	
The system should prompt the user to confirm the delivery address with the customer when an order is placed.	
The system should validate the postcode given by the customer on the PostCode Address File supplied by the Post Office.	
If the post code is not on the PostCode address file the user should be able to email the new postcode to the Post Office support desk.	
Any response from the Post Office support desk to this query should be put in the user's work-queue.	
The system should allow the user to update the billing address for the customer at the same time as the delivery address.	
The user should be able to disable the prompt to confirm the delivery address when there are a lot of customer calls waiting.	

The model answer is on the following page. Check you answer against that and – if there are significant discrepancies – go back and review the relevant sections, If you want a review of your answers email your answer to ISEBRE@smart-BA.com. There is a charge for this service - please pay online at http://www.smart-ba.com/purchase

ISEB Syllabus Section 2 exam style revision question MODEL ANSWER

Note: Your words and phrases do not have to be the same as the model answer, but the content should be similar.

Requirement	MODEL ANSWER
The system should be easier to use than the current system.	This requirement does not conform to the definition of a requirement. The phrase "easier to use than" is a measure (easiness of use) with a target ("than the current system") which means it could be an objective.
The system should prompt the user to confirm the delivery address with the customer when an order is placed.	Ok. Nothing much wrong with this. This requirement would appear to help achieve the objective "reduce the percentage of orders returned due incorrect delivery address by 66%"
The system should validate the postcode given by the customer on the PostCode Address File supplied by the Post Office.	There is an element of the solution in this requirement ("Postcode Address File") which may not be justified. Suggest amending the requirement to "The system should validate the postcode given by the customer." unless the solution is constrained to using this file for validation. Otherwise, this does
If the post code is not on the PostCode address file the user should be able to email the new postcode to the Post Office support desk.	There is an element of the solution in this requirement ("Postcode Address File") which may not be justified. This also applies to the use of the word "email". Perhaps amend requirement to "If the post code is invalid the user should be able to notify the Post Office support desk." This might contribute to project objectives in the long term (fixing addresses) but would need to confirm that as it would not help for that order.
Any response from the Post Office support desk to this query should be put in the user's work-queue.	The phrase "work queue" is ambiguous and needs to be defined. It is not clear how this requirement contributes to achieving project objectives.
The system should allow the user to update the billing address for the customer at the same time as the delivery address.	As a requirement it is ok, but it appears to be out of scope as it has nothing to do with the project objective of "reduce the percentage of orders returned due incorrect delivery address by 66%"

Questions? ISEBRE@smart-BA.com

Requirement	MODEL ANSWER
The user should be able to disable the prompt to confirm the delivery address when there are a lot of customer calls waiting.	As a requirement this is ok, but it appears to be in direct conflict with the earlier requirement to prompt the user to confirm the delivery address and would seem to actually reduce the solution's ability to achieve the project objective of "reduce the percentage of orders returned due incorrect delivery address by 66%"

©Guy Beauchamp 2009

Questions? ISEBRE@smart-BA.com

ISEB Syllabus Section 3 Hierarchy of Requirements

Key points:

1. The Business rationale – documents with such titles as Terms of Reference or Project Initiation Document (PID) – is everything that needs to be analysed in order to be able to establish that a project is worth doing (has benefits) and the scope of what it is doing in terms of what will change, where and who will be impacted. Any relevant risks, issues, dependencies, constraints are also defined.
2. There are the following types of requirements
   - General
   - Business
   - Functional
   - Non-functional
   - Technical
   - Data
   - Detailed

Detail:

1. The Business Rationale

The rationale for justifying the validity of project requirements is contained in a document that has various different names depending on approach being taken and the organisation standards – 2 very common names for this document are "Terms of Reference" (TOR) and "Project Initiation Document" (PID). Whatever it is called it will have certain information in it as shown in the following table:

Document Section	Notes	Example entry
Background	Sets the project in context and is typically written from the perspective of someone who knows nothing about the project but does know the business environment.	The IT department is running a project for the customer order delivery division of Ultimate Catalogue Company. This division is responsible for delivering orders from the company warehouse to the customer's delivery address. The issue facing the division is that around a third of these orders are being returned on first delivery attempt.
Objectives	Objectives are measures that can increased, decreased or maintained and if they hit a certain target value equate to project success.	Reduce the percentage of orders returned due incorrect delivery address – the target is 66%.
Scope	Defines the extent of the project's	Process: Record Sales Order

Questions? ISEBRE@smart-BA.com

Document Section	Notes	Example entry
	deliverables impact. Extents can be defined in lots of ways – POLDAT is a common starting point (**P**rocess, **O**rganisation, **L**ocation, **D**ata, **A**pplication, **T**echnology), but there can also be other extents and they can be combined in any way as well. A project can have many scoping definitions.	Organisation: Tele-Sales order team Location: Wetherfield Data: Delivery address Application: Ultimate Ordering System Technology: Ultimate Catalogue Company internal network
Specifically out of scope	Everything that is not defined as in scope is – by definition – out of scope. However, it is good practice to record anything that is debated and ruled out of scope along with who made the decision and why. This is used to justify why some requirements are excluded and saves having to re-have the discussion.	Process: Self-Record Sales Order (Web) Organisation: Customer Location: Anywhere Data: Delivery address Application: Ultimate On-Line Ordering System Technology: Ultimate Catalogue Company internet website Justification: the majority of errors are coming from the telesales order team, not customers on the website. Who was involved in this decision: A. Smith (project sponsor), B. Jones (project manager)
Constraints	Definition of what factors limit what can be done by the project (in the context of Requirements Engineering) in documenting requirements.	Requirements must be documented using the IT requirements templates.
Requirements	As defined in Section 2.	The system should prompt the user to confirm the delivery address with the customer when an order is placed.
Stakeholders	A list of who is involved and in what capacity in order to track who is generating and validating requirements.	A. Smith (project sponser) C. Gray (telesales order process subject matter expert)
Plan/Timescale	**Optional** section in that it is not required in order to justify the validity of the requirements. The overall project plan is typically owned and maintained by the Project Manager.	Target implementation date is 25th August 2010.
Budget	**Optional** section in that it is not required in order to justify the validity of the requirements. The overall project budget is typically owned and maintained by the Project Manager.	£50,000

©Guy Beauchamp 2009
Questions? ISEBRE@smart-BA.com

Document Section	Notes	Example entry
Business Case	**Optional** section in that it is not directly required in order to justify the validity of the requirements. Business Cases break down to benefits and costs. Benefits are the objectives. They are one and the same thing. This has already been documented. The only way they *may* be expressed differently here is to assign monetary value. Costs cannot be estimated with any accuracy until the solution in outline form is known. Only indicative costs can be estimated. The way these two figures are related to form a payback model vary by organisation.	Benefits: Reduce the percentage of orders returned due incorrect delivery address by 66% There are 250 delivery drivers making 2,500 deliveries a day of which around a third are wrong – 750 wrong deliveries a day. The project aim is to reduce this to 250 or less. Each wrong delivery costs £10, so the saving would be £5,000 per day. Costs: Changes to system, training and rollout estimated at £50,000. {organisation standard business case analysis}
Deliverables	What the project will produce and will persist after the project has closed down.	Changed Ultimate Order Taking System. Trained sales order team to use the new system capabilities.
Issues & Assumptions	Issues are factors outside of the project control that materially impede project progress, in this case related only to requirements engineering. Assumptions are made in order to allow work to continue even though an issue is impeding progress. The Project Manager normally has a central register of issues and assumptions and in that case only those that materially affect the requirements need to be included here.	Issue: There are insufficient Business Analysts to do the planned requirements analysis in the allotted time. Assumption: work will proceed on the assumption that more Business Analyst resource will be made available.
Risks	Risks are factors outside of the project control that could realistically occur and if they did would be issues that materially impede project progress, in this case related only to requirements engineering. The Project Manager normally has a central register of risks and in that case only those that materially affect the requirements need to be included here.	Not all requirements will be fully analysed if sufficient Business Analysis resource is not made available in the right time-frame.
Dependencies	Dependencies are factors outside of the project control which the project needs in	The project to improve capture of delivery address on the corporate

Questions? ISEBRE@smart-BA.com

Document Section	Notes	Example entry
	order to make progress, or which the project produces and another project cannot proceed without them. In either case only related only to requirements engineering. The Project Manager normally has a central register of risks and in that case only those that materially affect the requirements need to be included here.	website needs this project's requirements to define what a valid delivery address is before it can proceed.
Glossary	Any terms which could or have been mis-interpreted are defined in order to minimize ambiguity in the requirements.	*Delivery Address* is the UK postal address to which the goods ordered by the customer for a particular order are to be delivered. Notes: there is a default delivery address (see separate entry in this glossary) this is not necessarily the billing address.

The function of this document is to:
- document the requirements.
- document the other components of the project that will justify the validity of the requirements.

Questions? ISEBRE@smart-BA.com

2. Types of Requirements

There are 7 different categories of requirements. You can think of these different types of requirements as the answers to different types of questions that can be asked about the project requirements.

This first table shows the different types of requirements and the type of question about project requirements that they answer:

Requirement Type	Questions that this type of requirement answers	Example of this type of requirement
General	What is the overall scope of the project from a requirements perspective?	A solution is required that allows users to maintain customers and contact with those customers by salespeople.
Business	What specific capabilities must the whole solution deliver to the Business?	Users must be able to create a record of contact with a customer by a salesperson.
Functional	What specific capabilities must the computerised part of the solution deliver?	The system will provide the ability to record details of contacts with a customer by a salesperson.
Non-Functional	What requirements exist that do not fall in to any of the other categories?	The system must support up to 150 concurrent users.
Technical	What technical constraints must the solution abide by?	The system will be developed using object orientated standards.
Data	What rules must the data enforce?	A customer can have many contacts by a salesperson.
Detailed	What business rules are to be enforced by the solution?	A customer can not be deleted if they have had any contact with salespeople in the last 6 years.

This second table defines the different requirement categories and their use in Requirements Engineering:

Requirement Type	Definition	Uses
General	The highest level or broad statement of requirements or (rarely) a requirement that applies across all parts of the solution.	Used to describe the requirements scope a project. It is not definitive and will not subsequently be referenced by any other analysis component.
Business	A capability that the solution will deliver to the Business it did not have before with no unjustified elements of the solution.	Every Business Requirement will have one or more processes associated with it – and those processes are justified as being in scope by the fact that they relate to one or more Business or Functional requirements. Tests will be written and run that prove the capability has been delivered. Ideally, a Business requirement will have no elements of the solution whatsoever in it – if it does then it means that the requirement is scoped to the

Requirement Type	Definition	Uses
		extent of the solution that has been incorporated. Example: The requirement "be able to email the customer with confirmation of their appointment with a salesperson". If it is a constraint that the project must use email then this requirement is scoped to provide email functionality. If the project does not have to use email then this is an element of the solution that should be excluded: "be able to notify the customer with confirmation of their appointment with a salesperson". This allows other technical solutions such as SMS to be considered when it is time to design the solution.
Functional	Essentially the same as a Business requirement except that this being stated as a capability to be delivered by the computerised components of the solution.	Every Functional Requirement will have one or more processes associated with it – and those processes are justified as being in scope by the fact that they relate to one or more Business or Functional requirements. Tests will be written and run that prove the capability has been delivered. Ideally, a Functional requirement will also have no elements of the solution whatsoever in it (apart from the fact that it is the computerised solution that will deliver the capability) – if it does then it means that the requirement is scoped to the extent of the solution that has been incorporated. Example: The requirement "*The system shall* be able to email the customer with confirmation of their appointment with a salesperson". If it is a constraint that the project must use email then this requirement is scoped to provide email functionality. If the project does not have to use email then this is an element of the solution that should be excluded: "*The system shall* be able to notify the customer with confirmation of their appointment with a salesperson". This allows other technical solutions such as SMS to be considered when it is time to design the solution.
Non-Functional	There is no hard and fast definition of a non-functional requirement. In fact, even it's name only states what it is *not* rather than what it *is*.	Every project has non-functional requirements and they can relate to the whole solution and/or to processes and/or data. The usual ones are security (who can use which functionality) performance (how fast will the solution work)

Requirement Type	Definition	Uses
		availability (when is the solution useable) reliability (how often is it acceptable for the solution to fail or need maintenance) volumetrics (how many transactions, how many instances, predicted growth values and so on)
Technical	The technical constraints that the solution is required to conform to.	This has no further use in analysis of requirements but is crucial as soon as design work starts. Example: The solution will be developed using an Oracle DB.
Data	What information is needed to meet objectives and how it must relate to other information.	Data models will communicate definitive requirements for the data. There will be a two-way check between processes and data to prove that all the processes have all the information they need in order to be able to run and all the data is used by some processes somehow in order to meet project objectives.
Detailed	A rule that the business applies which must be part of the solution.	Rules can be expressed in many ways as there are many different types of rules: Process models define process dependency rules Process specifications define process execution rules Data models define data relationship rules Data specifications define data content rules Non-functional attributes of processes define security (who can do which processes) performance (how fast will the process work) service level agreements (when is the process useable) reliability (how often is it acceptable for the process to fail or need maintenance) volumetrics (how many transactions, predicted growth values and so on) Non-functional attributes of data define security (who can access which type of data) volumetrics (how many instances, predicted growth values etc)

Further Reading for Syllabus Section 3

Business Analysis – Debra Paul and Donald Yeates
Published by: The British Computer Society
ISBN 1-902505-70-0
Price: £20.00 from BCS and Amazon etc
Relevant Chapters/sections:
Chapter 9 – Requirements Engineering
    section The Problems With Requirements pages135-137 and
    section Requirements Analysis
    pages 147-149

Requirements Engineering by Gerald Kotonya and Ian Sommerville
Published by: John Willey & Sons
ISBN: 0-471-97208-8
Price: £36.00 from Amazon etc
Relevant Chapters/sections:
Chapter 8 – Non-Functional Requirements

For a slightly alternative view on requirements using slightly different terminology but the same concepts see
Business Analysis Body of Knowledge (BABOK) v1.6 from the International Institute of Business Analysts (IIBA) http://www.theiiba.org/AM/Template.cfm?Section=Body_of_Knowledge – free
Relevant Chapters/sections:
Chapter 5: requirements analysis and documentation

Writing Better Requirements by Ian F Alexander and Richard Stevens
Published by Addison-Wesley
ISBN 0-321-13163-0
Price £27.50 from Amazon etc
Relevant Chapters/sections:
    Chapter 1 Introduction

Questions? ISEBRE@smart-BA.com

ISEB Syllabus Section 3 exam style revision question

Ultimate Catalogue Company has initiated a project which has an objective to reduce the percentage of orders returned due incorrect delivery address by 66%.

The current process is that orders are taken, picked, packed and despatched from the warehouse to the customers delivery address. Customers can only have one delivery address at the moment and it is becoming more frequent for customers to want their orders delivering to a different address each time (presents etc). Sometimes the new address is taken but not recorded properly by the sales order team member who took it and sometimes it is just not taken at all. This is resulting in a significant proportion of failed deliveries due the order being delivered to the wrong or non-existent/incomplete address.

There are 250 delivery drivers making 2,500 deliveries a day of which around a third are wrong – 750 wrong deliveries a day.

The current solution has been developed on an Oracle platform and this is the strategic development platform for Ultimate Catalogue Company, so any changes must be made using this as the platform.

The main changes the business have identified are that it should be possible for one customer to have many delivery addresses and that each delivery address when it is created needs to be validated as much as possible – the most useful validation for the delivery drivers is house number or name and postcode. At the very least, every address must have a house name or number, and a postcode.

In order to minimise the risk of customer fraud only tele-sales order team personnel should have access to maintaining the delivery address.

Define 1 example requirement for each requirement type in the following table.

Requirement Type	Example Requirement
General requirement	
Business requirement	
Functional requirement	
Non-Functional requirement	
Technical requirement	
Data requirement	
Detailed requirement	

The model answer is on the following page. Check you answer against that and – if there are significant discrepancies – go back and review the relevant sections, If you want a review of your answers by a Business Analyst please complete the question and email your answer to ISEBRE@smart-BA.com. There is a charge for this service - please pay online at http://www.smart-ba.com/purchase

ISEB Syllabus Section 3 exam style revision question MODEL ANSWER

Requirement Type	Example Requirement
General requirement	Provide a solution that allows the telesales order team to capture and validate multiple delivery addresses for customer orders.
Business requirement	Be able to validate a delivery address.
Functional requirement	The system will validate a delivery address.
Non-Functional requirement	The system will be able to capture up to 2,500 delivery addresses per day.
Technical requirement	The solution must be developed on an Oracle platform.
Data requirement	One customer can have many delivery addresses.
Detailed requirement	A delivery address must have a postcode.

©Guy Beauchamp 2009

Questions? ISEBRE@smart-BA.com

ISEB Syllabus Section 4: Stakeholders in the Requirement Process

Key points:
- A stakeholder is any individual, group or organisation that can influence or impact the system under investigation.
- Stakeholder categorisation

Stakeholder	Category	Involvement in the Requirements Process
Sponsor	Business	Define problem or opportunity, initiate project, set objectives Define High Level Requirements Identify solution Sign-off Requirements
Domain Expert	Business	Define problem or opportunity, initiate project, set objectives Define High Level Requirements Define Low Level Detailed Requirements Identify solution Sign-off Requirements
Project Manager	Project	Define problem or opportunity, initiate project, set objectives Define High Level Requirements Identify solution Sign-off Requirements
End-User	Business	Define High Level Requirements Define Low Level Detailed Requirements Identify solution Sign-off Requirements
Business/Systems Analyst (Requirements Engineer)	Project	Define problem or opportunity, initiate project, set objectives Define High Level Requirements Define Low Level Detailed Requirements Identify solution Sign-off Requirements
Regulatory body	External	Define High Level Requirements Define Low Level Detailed Requirements
Legislative body	External	Define High Level Requirements Define Low Level Detailed Requirement
Customers	External	Define High Level Requirements Define Low Level Detailed Requirements
Suppliers	External	Define High Level Requirements Define Low Level Detailed Requirements
Programmer/Designer	Project	Designs solution based on signed-off Requirements

Stakeholder Detail:

Stakeholder	Category	Characteristics
Sponsor	Business	Sponsor commissions project Sets high level objectives Sets high level requirements Has power of acceptance or veto May not understand lower level needs Will agree Terms of Reference (Project Initiation Document).
Domain Expert	Business	Responsible for information on business domain Has broader view of problem area than end-user Has broader industry knowledge Can advise on what is feasible Can advise on what has worked or not worked before.
Project Manager	Project	Responsible for making sure the project progresses on schedule and within budget.
End-User	Business	Responsible for using system after delivery Will give low level requirements Will give many non-functional requirements Will test prototypes Must be involved in the requirements process.
Business/Systems Analyst (Requirements Engineer)	Project	Responsible for eliciting requirements Understands different elicitation techniques Responsible for negotiating between conflicting requirements Prepares accurate, clear requirements document.
Regulatory body	External	May be responsible for objectives for the project May be responsible for some High Level Requirements May be responsible for some Low Level Detailed Requirements
Legislative body	External	May be responsible for objectives for the project May be responsible for some High Level Requirements May be responsible for some Low Level Detailed Requirements
Customers	External	May be responsible for objectives for the project May be responsible for some High Level Requirements May be responsible for some Low Level Detailed Requirements
Suppliers	External	May be responsible for some High Level Requirements May be responsible for some Low Level Detailed Requirements
Programmer/Designer	Project	Will implement specified system Can advise on technical feasibility (especially non-functional requirements) Will build prototypes to test requirements Will advise on clarity of requirements.
Etc – there are many others but those listed above are the main ones		For example Testers will need to use requirements to generate test scripts, trainers will need to use requirements to design training programmes and so on.

Questions? ISEBRE@smart-BA.com

Further Reading for Syllabus Section 4

Business Analysis – Debra Paul and Donald Yeates
Published by: The British Computer Society
ISBN 1-902505-70-0
Price: £20.00 from BCS and Amazon etc
Relevant Chapters/sections:
Chapter 6 – Stakeholder Analysis and Management

Requirements Engineering by Gerald Kotonya and Ian Sommerville
Published by: John Willey & Sons
ISBN: 0-471-97208-8
Price: £36.00 from Amazon etc
Relevant Chapters/sections:
Chapter 2 – Requirements Engineering Processes
       Section 2.2. Actors in the Requirements Engineering Processes

For a slightly alternative view using slightly different terminology but the same concepts see
Business Analysis Body of Knowledge (BABOK) v1.6 from the International Institute of Business Analysts
(IIBA) http://www.theiiba.org/AM/Template.cfm?Section=Body_of_Knowledge – free
Relevant Chapters/sections:
3.2.2 TASK: Identify and Document Team Role Responsibilities and 3.2.3 Task: Identify Stakeholders

Writing Better Requirements by Ian F Alexander and Richard Stevens
Published by Addison-Wesley
ISBN 0-321-13163-0
Price £27.50 from Amazon etc
Relevant Chapters/sections:
       Chapter 2 Identifying the Stakeholders

ISEB Syllabus Section 4 exam style revision question

Mr A. Smith, Director of Customer Order Delivery Division at Ultimate Catalogue Company has initiated a project which has an objective to reduce the percentage of orders returned due incorrect delivery address by 66%. Mr Smith has assigned Ms. D. Bartlett as Project Manager.

According to Ms C. Gray (telesales order process domain expert) the current process is that orders are taken, picked, packed and despatched from the warehouse to the customers delivery address. Customers can only have one delivery address at the moment and it is becoming more frequent for customers to want their orders delivering to a different address each time (presents etc). Sometimes the new address is taken but not recorded properly by the sales order team member who took it and sometimes it is just not taken at all. This is resulting in a significant proportion of failed deliveries due the order being delivered to the wrong or non-existent/incomplete address.

There are 250 delivery drivers making 2,500 deliveries a day of which around a third are wrong – 750 wrong deliveries a day. These statistics have been produced by a Mr E. Clarke, a tele-sales order team member assigned to the project.

Mr B. Jones, the IT Director, has stated that the current solution has been developed on an Oracle platform and this is the strategic development platform for Ultimate Catalogue Company, so any changes must be made using this as the platform.

With the help of the Business Analyst Ms. F. Harrison, the main changes the business have identified are that it should be possible for one customer to have many delivery addresses and that each delivery address when it is created needs to be validated as much as possible – the most useful validation for the delivery drivers is house number or name and postcode. At the very least, every address must have a house name or number, and a postcode.

The project has been informed by Mr. H. Mannering from the Internal Audit and QA Dept that in order to minimise the risk of customer fraud only tele-sales order team personnel should have access to maintaining the delivery address. This is a company standard adopted in line with the Mail Order Fraud Prevention Scheme sponsored by the UK Government.

Using the table below, identify the stakeholders, their category and at what point you think they should be involved in the Requirements Process.

Stakeholder name	Stakeholder Type	Category	Involvement in the Requirements Process

Questions? ISEBRE@smart-BA.com

Stakeholder name	Stakeholder Type	Category	Involvement in the Requirements Process

If you want a review of your answers by a Business Analyst please complete the question and email your answer to ISEBRE@smart-BA.com. There is a charge for this service - please pay online at http://www.smart-ba.com/purchase

ISEB Syllabus Section 4 exam style revision question MODEL ANSWER

Stakeholder	Stakeholder Type	Category	Involvement in the Requirements Process
Mr A Smith	Sponsor	Business	Define problem or opportunity, initiate project, set objectives Define High Level Requirements Identify solution Sign-off Requirements
Ms D Bartlett	Project Manager	Project	Define problem or opportunity, initiate project, set objectives Define High Level Requirements Identify solution Sign-off Requirements
Ms C Gray	Domain Expert	Business	Define problem or opportunity, initiate project, set objectives Define High Level Requirements Define Low Level Detailed Requirements Identify solution Sign-off Requirements
Mr E Clarke	End user	Business	Define High Level Requirements Define Low Level Detailed Requirements Identify solution Sign-off Requirements
Mr B Jones	Domain Expert	Business	Define problem or opportunity, initiate project, set objectives Define High Level Requirements Define Low Level Detailed Requirements Identify solution Sign-off Requirements
Ms F Harrison	Business/Systems Analyst (Requirements Engineer)	Project	Define problem or opportunity, initiate project, set objectives Define High Level Requirements Define Low Level Detailed Requirements Identify solution Sign-off Requirements
Mr H Mannering	Regulatory body	External	Define High Level Requirements Define Low Level Detailed Requirements

ISEB Syllabus Section 5: Requirements Elicitation
Key points:

- There are the following types of knowledge:

Knowledge Type	Description
Explicit	knowledge that can be communicated using just words.
Tacit	knowledge that comes from experience and judgment.
Semi-Tacit	knowledge that is assumed everyone knows – also known as 'common sense', 'obvious'.
Future Systems	what is predicted will be true in the new 'green field' system.

- There are the following ways of eliciting knowledge

Elicitation Technique	Description
Interviews	1 person is interviewed by 1 one or more Business Analysts who control and direct the interview.
Workshops	More than 1 person who work together to uncover some knowledge or make a decision. May be facilitated by a Business Analyst.
Observation	Business Analysts should be observing all the time and spotting issues, opportunities, etc.
Shadowing	Business Analyst does the job under user supervision.
Ethnographic Study	Business Analyst does the job for a long time initially under user supervision but eventually becoming a user for the duration of the study (typically months)
Prototyping – see section 9 for further detail	A mock-up of the solution is developed by the Business Analyst to trial the requirements.
Scenarios	Business Analysts work with one or more users through requirements for all the different combinations of factors that result in a different route through all the processes.
Protocol Analysis	Business Analyst documents the thought processes of an Expert (they provide a running commentary) as they carry out a process.
Document Analysis	Record Searching (i.e. the archives) to establish volumes, frequencies and trends in data. Inspecting individual documents to gain an understanding of the data used by the business meaning and usage of data items information requirements for the future.
Special Purpose records	A way of capturing very simple information (usually just a count) about certain transactions.

©Guy Beauchamp 2009
Questions? ISEBRE@smart-BA.com

Elicitation Technique	Description
Questionnaires	A way of capturing more complex information about certain transactions or general views, opinions and ideas.
Sampling	Statistical Sampling is used to confirm estimates, can involve record searching special purpose records. BAs should involve a statistician if the results are important for statistics expertise. Activity sampling used when high volume or time involved makes thorough observation impossible.
Reverse engineering	If all else fails, deconstruct the existing solution code to determine what requirements are being satisfied.

Questions? ISEBRE@smart-BA.com

ISEB Certificate in Requirements Engineering
Self Study 'JEEP' Manual

- This table shows which elicitation techniques are appropriate for which knowledge types
  - √√ = very useful
  - √ = useful
  - X = Does not help

Elicitation Technique	Suitable for eliciting knowledge types			
	Explicit	Tacit	Semi Tacit	Future systems
Interviews	√√	√	√	√√
Workshops	√√	√	√	√√
Observation	√	√√	√√	X
Shadowing	√	√√	√√	X
Ethnographic Study	X	√√	√√	X
Prototyping	√√	√	√√	√
Scenarios	√√	√	√	√
Protocol Analysis	√√	√√	√√	X
Document Analysis	X	√	√	X
Special Purpose records	√√	X	X	X
Questionnaires	√√	X	X	X
Sampling	√	X	X	X
Reverse engineering	√	X	X	X

Details:

Knowledge Type details

Knowledge	Description
Explicit	Information that can be got through conversation, interview and questioning. Example: Are only UK addresses in scope?
Tacit	Sort of knowledge that a doctor uses to diagnose patients. This knowledge is built up from years of training and experience and cannot easily be conveyed verbally. Example: try explaining verbally how to maintain your balance on a bicycle.
Semi-Tacit	What everyone assumes everyone else knows. Major source of errors for Business Analysts as the users will assume that the Business Analyst knows this information and (worse) the Business Analyst might assume they know it as well but they don't! Example: Obviously, everyone knows difference between red and green. This example shows the dangers of semi-tacit knowledge: if you have a certain type of colour blindness you don't know the difference and this is why some colour blind people cannot be airline pilots.
Future Systems	Only applies to brand new systems where there was no pre-existing solution that is being changed or replaced: it is a 'green field' development. The knowledge is what users and other stakeholders think they know about the new system – they are their predictions for what will be true after the new system has been implemented. Example: The brand new 'green field' system for recording sales orders for a new company. There are no existing systems so it is a 'green field' development.

Elicitation Technique Details

Elicitation Technique	Description
Interviews	The most common form of elicitation technique for Business Analysts. Treat each interview as a 'mini project': define objectives for the interview (e.g. increase your knowledge about postcode validation) and then plan your interview questions around that. Use open questions to elicit the information (an open question is a question that cannot easily be answered 'yes' or 'no'. E.g.: please tell me how you want the postcode to be validated.). Used closed questions to confirm information (a closed question is one that can easily be answered 'yes' or 'no'. E.g. So the first stage of validating the postcode is to check it exists on the Post Office Address File?). The structure of the interview should be: 1. introduce yourself, why you are there and explain the format of the interview. 2. ask open questions to elicit the information. 3. ask closed questions to confirm your understanding. 4. explain next steps – and how the interviewee will be involved. 5. ask them if they have any questions. 6. thank them and close interview.
Workshops	If you need to interview more than one person at once then this is a workshop. As a Business Analyst, you will need to hold a workshop if • you need to get a decision made involving many people and/or organisation units. • you need to define requirements that will impact many organisation units. • workshops can also be held to establish/affirm teams. The structure of the workshop is roughly the same for an interview.
Observation	This is a passive activity that Business Analysts should always be doing: observing their environment and noting issues and opportunities as well as discovering how processes work and what data they need to work.
Shadowing	A Business Analyst can learn more effectively about a role they are analysing if they actually do the job. Usually this will be under user supervision as the Analyst will have no formal training or qualifications for that role.
Ethnographic Study	A Business Analyst does the job for a long time initially under user supervision but eventually becoming a user for the duration of the study (typically months). The idea is that actually becoming a user allows the Business Analyst to spot issues and opportunities from a BA perspective as well as thoroughly understanding the role in detail. This is rarely used as a technique in real life due to the cost/time investment.
Prototyping – see section 9 for further detail	A mock-up of the solution is developed by the Business Analyst to trial the requirements. The mock up can range from drawing up how the solution will look on paper to a fully functional 'system'. We will cover this is more detail in Syllabus Section 9.
Scenarios	Business Analysts work with one or more users through requirements for all the

Questions? ISEBRE@smart-BA.com

Elicitation Technique	Description
	different combinations of factors that result in a different route through a process. For example, the way the process to record the delivery address works will be different for the scenario where a customer lives at an address that has a valid postcode and the scenario where a customer lives at an address that has an invalid postcode.
Protocol Analysis	Business Analyst documents the thought processes of an Expert (they provide a running commentary) as they carry out a process. Experimental evidence has shown that self-reports can access cognitive processes that cannot be fully recalled without bias and distortion if explained after the task has been completed. Example: the user explains "the postcode is invalid so I ask the customer if they are living in a new build house as they may have a postcode that has not be notified to us yet."
Document Analysis	Record Searching (i.e. the archives) to establish volumes, frequencies and trends in data. Inspecting individual documents to gain an understanding of the data used by the business meaning and usage of data items information requirements for the future. This means going back through historical data either physically or electronically to find out definitive answers to specific questions. Example: use document analysis to find out how often postcodes fail validation and whether this is increasing in frequency.
Special Purpose records	A way of capturing very simple information (usually just a count) about certain transactions. Example: get telesales order team to keep a count of how often postcodes are invalid because the customer lives in a new-build house with a new postcode that has been notified to them yet.
Questionnaires	A way of capturing more complex information about certain transactions or general views, opinions and ideas. Example: Get the telesales order team to record the different reasons they have come across for invalid postcodes and whether they can think of any solutions to these errors.
Sampling	Statistical Sampling is used to confirm estimates, can involve record searching special purpose records. BAs should involve a statistician if the results are important for statistics expertise. Activity sampling used when high volume or time involved makes thorough observation impossible. Example: rather than search through the 5,000,000 orders that have been taken since trading began 25 years ago, take 100 orders from each year of trading to build up a picture of standard orders.
Reverse engineering	If all else fails, deconstruct the existing solution code to determine what requirements are being satisfied. This can be used when there is no documentation about the solution and nobody remembers how it is meant to work. Normally relevant for specific business rules rather than overall processes. Example: how does the current system work out if the telesales team member is placing an order for themselves (which is not allowed).

Questions? ISEBRE@smart-BA.com

ISEB Certificate in Requirements Engineering

Self Study 'JEEP' Manual

The following table shows which for each project stage what analysis products are produced, which stakeholders to involve, what type of knowledge is involved and what elicitation technique is appropriate

Project Stage	Analysis Product	Stakeholder	Knowledge Type	Elicitation Technique
Project Definition	Objectives	Sponsor Anyone who is authorised to make go/no go decisions on the project	Explicit	Interview Workshop
High Level Requirements	High Level Requirements	Sponsor Project Manager Domain Expert Anyone who is authorised to make go/no go decisions on the project	Explicit	Workshop
			Tacit	Workshop Observation
			Semi-Tacit	Workshop Observation
			Future System	Workshop
Detailed Requirements	Process models & specifications Data models & specifications Business non-functional rules	Domain experts Users	Explicit	Interviews Workshops Observation Shadowing Prototyping Scenarios Protocol Analysis Special Purpose Records Questionnaires Sampling Reverse Engineering
			Tacit	Interviews Observation Shadowing Ethnographic Studies Prototyping Scenarios Protocol Analysis Document Analysis

©Guy Beauchamp 2009

Questions? ISEBRE@smart-BA.com

Project Stage	Analysis Product	Stakeholder	Knowledge Type	Elicitation Technique
			Semi-tacit	Interviews Observation Shadowing Ethnographic Studies Prototyping Scenarios Protocol Analysis Document Analysis
			Future System	Interviews Ethnographic studies Prototyping Scenarios

©Guy Beauchamp 2009

Questions? ISEBRE@smart-BA.com

Further Reading for Syllabus Section 5

Business Analysis – Debra Paul and Donald Yeates
Published by: The British Computer Society
ISBN 1-902505-70-0
Price: £20.00 from BCS and Amazon etc
Relevant Chapters/sections:
Chapter 5 – Investigation Techniques
Also "Business Knowledge" p 18

For a slightly alternative view using slightly different terminology but the same concepts see
Business Analysis Body of Knowledge (BABOK) v1.6 from the International Institute of Business Analysts
(IIBA) http://www.theiiba.org/AM/Template.cfm?Section=Body_of_Knowledge – free
Relevant Chapters/sections:
Chapter 4 Requirements Elicitation

Questions? ISEBRE@smart-BA.com

ISEB Syllabus Section 5 exam style revision question

Mr A. Smith, Director of Customer Order Delivery Division at Ultimate Catalogue Company has initiated a project which has an objective to reduce the percentage of orders returned due incorrect delivery address by 66%. Mr Smith has assigned Ms. D. Bartlett as Project Manager.

According to Ms C. Gray (telesales order process subject matter expert) the current process is that orders are taken, picked, packed and despatched from the warehouse to the customers delivery address. Customers can only have one delivery address at the moment and it is becoming more frequent for customers to want their orders delivering to a different address each time (presents etc). Sometimes the new address is taken but not recorded properly by the sales order team member who took it and sometimes it is just not taken at all. This is resulting in a significant proportion of failed deliveries due the order being delivered to the wrong or non-existent/incomplete address.

There are 250 delivery drivers making 2,500 deliveries a day of which around a third are wrong – 750 wrong deliveries a day. These statistics have been produced by a Mr E. Clarke, a tele-sales order team member assigned to the project.

Mr B. Jones, the IT Director, has stated that the current solution has been developed on an Oracle platform and this is the strategic development platform for Ultimate Catalogue Company, so any changes must be made using this as the platform.

With the help of the Business Analyst Ms. F. Harrison, the main changes the business have identified are that it should be possible for one customer to have many delivery addresses and that each delivery address when it is created needs to be validated as much as possible – the most useful validation for the delivery drivers is house number or name and postcode. At the very least, every address must have a house name or number, and a postcode.

The project has been informed by Mr. H. Mannering from the Internal Audit and QA Dept that in order to minimise the risk of customer fraud only tele-sales order team personnel should have access to maintaining the delivery address. This is a company standard adopted in line with the Mail Order Fraud Prevention Scheme sponsored by the UK Government.

You have been tasked with analysing the High Level Requirements and Detailed Requirements for this project.

State what elicitation techniques you are going to use and with who to complete these tasks.

If you want a review of your answers by a Business Analyst please complete the question and email your answer to ISEBRE@smart-BA.com. There is a charge for this service - please pay online at http://www.smart-ba.com/purchase

ISEB Certificate in Requirements Engineering
Self Study 'JEEP' Manual

ISEB Syllabus Section 5 exam style revision question MODEL ANSWER

High Level Requirements	Mr Sponsor – Mr A Smith Project Manager – Ms D Bartlett Domain Expert – Ms C Gray Domain Expert – Mr B Jones Regulatory Body – Mr H Mannering	Workshop Observation
Detailed Requirements	Domain Expert – Ms C Gray Domain Expert – Mr B Jones Regulatory Body – Mr H Mannering End user – Mr E Clarke	Interviews Workshops Observation Shadowing Prototyping Scenarios Protocol Analysis Special Purpose Records Questionnaires Sampling Reverse Engineering

NB: Make sure you reference the names for the relevant roles from the scenario otherwise you can be marked down for giving what is referred to as "text book" answer – an answer you could have copied verbatim out of one the books you have been allowed to take in to the exam.

©Guy Beauchamp 2009
Questions? ISEBRE@smart-BA.com

ISEB Syllabus Section 6: Use of Models in Requirements Engineering
Key points:

This is the largest section in the syllabus.

There are two fundamental sets of models required to fully define requirements:
1. Process models
2. Data models

This is not surprising given that any solution computerised or not consists of a set of processes manipulating a set of data.

In the ISEB Certificate in Requirements Engineering you are required to be able to **build** a process model but only **read** a data model.

A process model defines dependencies between process steps.
The process specification defines the execution logic that the process implements.
Every process will have a set of non-functional requirements defined as well.

A data model defines the relationships between entities.
Data attribute specification defines what the entities need to be able to store in terms of information.
Every entity will have a set of non-functional requirements defined as well.

Detail:
Process models.
We will use Business Process Modelling Notation (BPMN) as this is the industry standard. You are allowed to use almost any notation standard you like that is a recognized standard, with the exception of Data Flow Diagrams which are no longer allowed.

BPMN is an extensive notation set but we will focus on those you need in order to pass the exam. See the "Further Reading" section for details on further notation. BPMN is also useful for the ISEB Certificate in Modelling Business Processes.

BPMN process models consist of symbols for different types of
- swimlane
- activities
- events
- gateways
- flows

The following table shows the different symbol types and their meaning (all definitions taken from http://www.bpmn.org/Documents/BPMN%201-1%20Specification.pdf and http://www.modernanalyst.com/Resources/Templates/tabid/146/articleType/ArticleView/articleId/487/Default.aspx)

Type of symbol	Symbol name	Symbol	Description
Swimlane			A Swimlane is a graphical container for partitioning a set of activities from other activities. BPMN has two different types of Swimlanes.
	Pool	Pool	A Pool represents a Participant in a Process. It also acts as a "swimlane" and a graphical container for partitioning a set of activities from other Pools, usually in the context of B2B situations. It is a square-cornered rectangle that is drawn with a solid single line. A Pool acts as the container for the Sequence Flow between activities. The Sequence Flow can cross the boundaries between Lanes of a Pool, but cannot cross the boundaries of a Pool. The interaction between Pools, e.g., in a B2B context, is shown through Message Flow.

Questions? ISEBRE@smart-BA.com

Type of symbol	Symbol name	Symbol	Description
	Lane	A diagram showing a Pool containing a Lane, divided into two horizontal sections	A Lane is a sub-partition within a Pool and will extend the entire length of the Pool, either vertically or horizontally. Lanes are used to organize and categorize activities within a Pool. The meaning of the Lanes is up to the modeller.
Activity			**Always named Verb phrase+Nown phrase: do something to something. Marks are deducted for failure to follow this simple rule.** An activity is a generic term for work that a company or organization performs via business processes. An activity can be atomic or non-atomic (compound). The types of activities that are a part of a Process Model are: Process, Sub-Process, and Task.
	Process	Process	A Process is any activity performed within a company or organization. In BPMN a Process is depicted as a network of Flow Objects, which are a set of other activities and the controls that sequence them.
	Sub-process	Collapsed sub-process [+]	A Sub-Process is a Process that is included within another Process. The Sub-Process can be in a collapsed view that hides its details. A Sub-Process can be in an expanded view that shows its details within the view of the Process in which it is contained. A Sub-Process shares the same shape as the Task, which is a rectangle that has rounded corners.

Type of symbol	Symbol name	Symbol	Description
	Task	Task	A Task is an atomic activity that is included within a Process. A Task is used when the work in the Process is not broken down to a finer level of Process Model detail. Generally, an end-user and/or an application are used to perform the Task when it is executed. A Task object shares the same shape as the Sub-Process, which is a rectangle that has rounded corners.
	Iteration	Process ↺ Task ↺ Collapsed sub-process ↺ [+]	To show that a process, sub-process or task can be performed 1 thru 'n' times defined by the processing logic in the iteration object.
Event			An event is one of: • something that occurs externally to the solution that the solution has to respond to • the solution produces as output and that product leaves the scope of the solution • the solution terminates.
	Start event	Start Event – no trigger Start Event – message trigger Start Event – rules trigger Start Event – timer trigger Start Event – link trigger	A Start Event indicates where a particular Process will start. In terms of Sequence Flow, the Start Event starts the flow of the Process, and thus will not have any incoming Sequence Flow. A Start Event can have a Trigger that indicates how the Process starts: Message, Timer, Rule, Link. The Start Event shares the same basic shape of the Intermediate Event and End Event, a circle, but is drawn with a single thin line.

Questions? ISEBRE@smart-BA.com

Type of symbol	Symbol name	Symbol	Description
	Intermediate event	intermediate Event – no trigger / intermediate Event – message trigger / intermediate Event – rules trigger / intermediate Event – timer trigger / intermediate Event – link trigger	An Intermediate Event is an event that occurs after a Process has been started. It will affect the flow of the process, but will not start or (directly) terminate the process. An Intermediate Event will show where messages or delays are expected within the Process, disrupt the Normal Flow through exception handling, or show the extra flow required for compensating a transaction. The Intermediate Event shares the same basic shape of the Start Event and End Event, a circle, but is drawn with a thin double line.
	End event	End Event – no result / End Event – message sent / End Event – terminate / End Event – link	As the name implies, the End Event indicates where a process will end. In terms of Sequence Flow, the End Event ends the flow of the Process, and thus, will not have any outgoing Sequence Flow. An End Event can have a specific Result that will appear as a marker within the center of the End Event shape. The End Event shares the same basic shape of the Start Event and Intermediate Event, a circle, but is drawn with a thick single line
Gateway			A Gateway is used to control the divergence and convergence of Sequence Flow. Thus it will determine branching, forking, merging, and joining of paths. Internal markers will indicate the type of behavior control. There are five types of gateways.
	Exclusive or	Xor condition / Xor condition	Data-Based exclusive decision and merging. Shown with or without the "X" marker – i.e. the default is Xor.

Questions? ISEBRE@smart-BA.com

Type of symbol	Symbol name	Symbol	Description
	Inclusive or	◇○ *Inclusive or condition*	Inclusive decision and merging
	And	◇+ *And condition*	Simultaneous forking or joining
	Complex	◇✳ *Complex condition*	Complex conditions and situations (e.g., 3 out of 5 times go one way, 2 times out of 5 go the other)
	Event based gateway	◇⊛ *(this symbol is not named)*	An "exclusive or" decision made on the basis of whichever associated intermediate event occurs first.
Flow			A Flow is a graphical line connecting two objects in a BPMN diagram. There are two types of Flow: Sequence Flow and Message Flow, each with their own line style. Flow is also used in a generic sense (and lowercase) to describe how Tokens will traverse Sequence Flow from the Start Event to an End Event.
	Sequence flow	→	Flow that proceeds, unrestricted, from one Flow Object to another, via a Sequence Flow link, without any dependencies on another flow or any conditional expressions. Typically, this is seen as a Sequence flow between two activities, without a conditional indicator (mini-diamond) or any intervening Gateway.

©Guy Beauchamp 2009
Questions? ISEBRE@smart-BA.com

Type of symbol	Symbol name	Symbol	Description
	Sequence flow with condition	◇—Condition name—▶	Flow that proceeds from one Flow Object to another, via a Sequence Flow link, but is subject to either conditions or dependencies from other flow as defined by a Gateway. Typically, this is seen as a Sequence flow between two activities, with a conditional indicator (mini-diamond) or a Sequence Flow connected to a Gateway.
	Message flow	○----Message flow name----▷	A Message Flow is a dashed line that is used to show the flow of messages between two entities that are prepared to send and receive them. In BPMN, two separate Pools in the Diagram will represent the two entities.
	Data Object	Data Object 1	In BPMN, a Data Object is considered an Artefact and not a Flow Object. They are considered an Artefact because they do not have any direct affect on the Sequence Flow or Message Flow of the Process, but they do provide information about what the Process does. That is, how documents, data, and other objects are used and updated during the Process. While the name "Data Object" may imply an electronic document, they can be used to represent many different types of objects, both electronic and physical.
Text annotation		Annotation text	Can be applied to any object on a BPMN diagram to add clarity. Is for communication purposes only and does not form part of the specification.

Questions? ISEBRE@smart-BA.com

Have a look at the following example process model. You should be able to read and understand how the process
- starts
- who is involved with the process
- what processes it goes through
- under what conditions which flows will be followed
- how it terminates

The business process being modeled is customer query handling by 1st and 2nd line support teams, who use an external agency to solve technical queries.

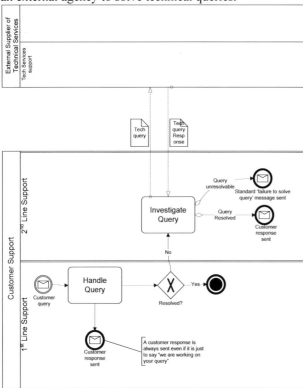

Notes:
1. There is an xor gateway called 'resolved' which does essentially the same job as the two conditional flows coming from "investigate query". The only difference is that although you would expect the two conditional flows to be mutually exclusive the diagram does not enforce the rule – conditional flows will be followed when the conditions are satisfied and two conditions could be satisfied at once (see next example).
2. The default for BPMN for flows leaving a process, sub-process or task is that they all leave at the same time unless there is some rule in the diagram that says they cannot – in the example above the

process flow from "handle query" to "customer response sent" and to the gateway "resolved?" both occur as that process step concludes.

Some more notes about BPMN usage:
Consider the following process

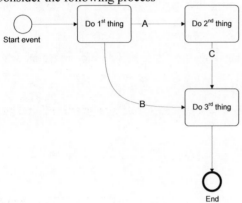

The task "Do 1st Thing" has 2 flows (A and B) leaving it. As both flows are unconditional flows, these would be followed unconditionally *and simultaneously* every time.

The task "Do 3rd Thing" has 2 flows (A and C) coming in to it. The default notation for BPMN is that **either** flow A **or** flow C can trigger the task.

If you wanted to show the business rule that flows A **and** C are required before the task can start you would show it like this:

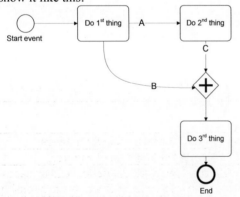

Process breaks:

There is a process break between "Do 1st Thing" and "Do 2nd Thing". That break comes to an end when the intermediate event "message received" occurs.

Questions? ISEBRE@smart-BA.com

Suppose the business rule is that the message must be received within 3 days or the process stops:

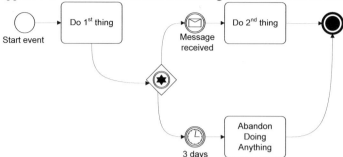

Note the use of the event based gateway. It shows that there is a process break here which will end when one of any number of events occurs.

There are plenty more examples of process models in the reading list.

Data models.
We will use Entity Relationship Diagrams (ERD) as this is the most widely used. In the ISEB exam you are not required to be able to create a data model, just read one.

A data model consists of entities related to each other on a diagram:

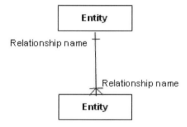

Data model element	Definition
Entity	A real world thing or an interaction between 2 or more real world things.
Attribute	The atomic pieces of information that we need to know about entities.
Relationship	How entities depend on each other in terms of why the entities depend on each other (the relationship) and what that relationship is (the cardinality of the relationship).

Example:
"Customer" is an entity.
"Product" is an entity.
For a "Customer" we need to know their "customer number" attribute and "name" attribute.
For a "Product" we need to know the "product name" attribute and "price" attribute.
"Sale" is an entity that is used to record the interaction of "Customer" and "Product".
Here is the diagram:

ISEB Certificate in Requirements Engineering
Self Study 'JEEP' Manual

Notes:

1. By convention, entities are named in the singular.
2. the attributes of "Customer" are "Customer No" (which is the unique identifier or primary key of the "Customer" entity and is shown by the # symbol) and "Customer Name".
3. "Sale" has a composite primary key made up of the primary key of "Customer", the primary key of "Product" and the date of the sale.
4. Think of entities as tables, think of attributes as columns on the table and think of instances as rows on that table:

Customer *(entity)*

Customer No *(attribute)*	Customer Name *(attribute)*	
10	Fred Bloggs	*(instance)*
67	Freda Jones	*(attribute)*

Sale

Customer No	Product Name	Date
10	101	21/2/2020
67	452	22/2/2020

Product

Product Name	Price
101	£123.00
452	£34.50

5. If we want to know the price of a Sale, we can 'find' it by using the "Product Name" on the instance of "Sale" we are interested in and look up the corresponding "Price" on the "Product" entity with the matching "Product Name".

Cardinality.

©Guy Beauchamp 2009

Questions? ISEBRE@smart-BA.com

This term refers to what the relationship dependency is and the valid set of cardinalities is shown here:

Crows Foot Cardinality

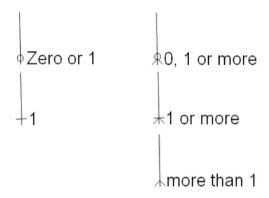

Zero or 1

0, 1 or more

1

1 or more

more than 1

This is known as crows foot notation. There are other notations such as UML Class Associations:

UML Class Cardinality

o | Zero

1 | 1

o...'n' | 0, 1 or more

1...'n' | 1 or more

'n'...'n' | more than 1

Whatever notation, cardinality is defined at both ends of a relationship and in any combination.

Cardinality refers to the entity that it is closest to.

Reading a data model.

Relationships are read by building a sentence:

        a. Name the entity where you are starting from in the singular: "Each Customer"
          (Note: entity names by convention start with an upper case letter).
        b. Read the name of the relationship you are reading and put it in to a sentence: "purchases"

(Note: the end of the relationship the name is at is arbitrary: construct the best sentence you can in context of the requirements as you understand them).

  c. Read the cardinality of the end of the relationship you are reading: "1 or more"

  d. Name the entity you are ending up on in the singular or plural depending on the cardinality at that end of the relationship: "Sales".

All together this makes: "One Customer purchases one or more Sales". In this case as the Customer must purchase at least one sale you can (and should) include this in the sentence: "One Customer **must** purchase one or more Sales". If the Customer did not have to purchase any Sales to be a Customer then the sentence would be "One Customer **may** purchase zero, one or more Sales".

You only need to be able to read a data model for the ISEB exam. When you are reading a data model like this you have to be able to contextualise it in terms of requirements that are being satisfied by the data model. So, in the example we have of "One Customer must purchase one or more Sales" we would want to be sure that this *is* the business rule.

Example reading of a data model:

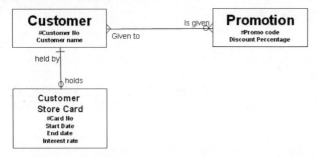

1. Each Customer may be given zero, 1 or more Promotions. (Note: the use of the word 'may' here indicates that this is an optional relationship in that the customer may have zero Promotions or one or many Promotions).

2. Each Promotion must be given to more than 1 Customers. (Note: the use of the word 'must' here indicates that the relationship is mandatory: if a Promotion exists then it must be given to more than 1 Customer).

3. Each Customer may hold zero or 1 Customer Store Cards.

4. Each Customer Store Card must be held by 1 Customer.

Notes:

1. **Always** use the full name of the entity at each end of the relationship you are reading.

2. **Always** use 'may' for relationships that have the option of zero for the target entity.

3. **Always** use 'must' for relationships that do not have the option of zero for the target entity.

4. **Always** use the relationship name (if there is one) or create one from what you know of the requirements.

5. **Always** make sure that the relationship name represents a business requirement.

6. The sentences should be grammatical.

7. Sense check: would you predict a business representative would be able to validate the sentence you construct from the data model as being a business requirement?

8. **Never** use database design terminology (this is a definition of requirements for data, not a design for a database!).

Questions? ISEBRE@smart-BA.com

ISEB Certificate in Requirements Engineering

Self Study 'JEEP' Manual

Further Reading for Syllabus Section 6

Process modelling
Business Analysis – Debra Paul and Donald Yeates
Published by: The British Computer Society
ISBN 1-902505-70-0
Price: £20.00 from BCS and Amazon etc
Relevant Chapters/sections:
Chapter 8 – Business Process Modelling.

http://www.modernanalyst.com/Resources/Templates/tabid/146/articleType/ArticleView/articleId/487/Cheat-Sheet-for-BPMN-Business-Process-Modelling-Notation.aspx – a great BPMN reminder sheet to take in to the exam.

BPMN1.1. http://www.bpmn.org/Documents/BPMN%201-1%20Specification.pdf – free
Section 11 – BPMN by example for extended model – note that this contains some notation we have not covered as it is not required for the exam.

http://www.bpmn.org/exampleIndex.htm - a set of example BPMN diagrams – note that these contain some notation we have not covered as it is not required for the exam.

http://www.businessprocesstrends.com/publicationfiles/07-04%20WP%20Intro%20to%20BPMN%20-%20White.pdf a good introduction from Stephen White who is on the OMG that controls BPMN with a discussion at the end about where BPMN may evolve to.

Data modelling:
Business Analysis – Debra Paul and Donald Yeates
Published by: The British Computer Society
ISBN 1-902505-70-0
Price: £20.00 from BCS and Amazon etc
Relevant Chapters/sections:
Chapter 10 – Modelling the IT System section Modelling System Data on p 162-176.
Also Chapter 11 Managing the Information Resource for a more all round discussion on data issues p 177-194

For a detailed consideration of data modelling see
Business Analysis Body of Knowledge (BABOK) v1.6 from the International Institute of Business Analysts (IIBA) http://www.theiiba.org/AM/Template.cfm?Section=Body_of_Knowledge – free
Relevant Chapters/sections:
Appendix 5.12 Technique: Data and Behavior Models p 211 onwards

©Guy Beauchamp 2009
Questions? ISEBRE@smart-BA.com

ISEB Syllabus Section 6 exam style revision question – process model

Mr A. Smith, Director of Customer Order Delivery Division at Ultimate Catalogue Company has initiated a project which has an objective to reduce the percentage of orders returned due incorrect delivery address by 66%. Mr Smith has assigned Ms. D. Bartlett as Project Manager.

According to Ms C. Gray (telesales order process subject matter expert) the current process is that orders are taken, picked, packed and despatched from the warehouse to the customers delivery address. Customers can only have one delivery address at the moment and it is becoming more frequent for customers to want their orders delivering to a different address each time (presents etc). Sometimes the new address is taken but not recorded properly by the sales order team member who took it and sometimes it is just not taken at all. This is resulting in a significant proportion of failed deliveries due the order being delivered to the wrong or non-existent/incomplete address.

There are 250 delivery drivers making 2,500 deliveries a day of which around a third are wrong – 750 wrong deliveries a day. These statistics have been produced by a Mr E. Clarke, a tele-sales order team member assigned to the project.

Mr B. Jones, the IT Director, has stated that the current solution has been developed on an Oracle platform and this is the strategic development platform for Ultimate Catalogue Company, so any changes must be made using this as the platform.

With the help of the Business Analyst Ms. F. Harrison, the main changes the business have identified are that it should be possible for one customer to have many delivery addresses and that each delivery address when it is created needs to be validated as much as possible – the most useful validation for the delivery drivers is house number or name and postcode. At the very least, every address must have a house name or number, and a postcode.

The way that the business would like the amendments to the process to work is that at the point of ordering the telesales advisor is prompted to ask the customer what delivery address they would like the order to be sent to. The prompt should suggest the use of the customers' default delivery address. If the customer specifies another address then the advisor should look this address up for the customer. If the address exists then the advisor should associate that address to the order. If the address does not exist then the advisor should capture the full address details (as a minimum it should have the house name or number, postcode and post town) and – after being validated (the business is not sure what the validation rules are yet) – this new address should be associated with the order.

The project has been informed by Mr. H. Mannering from the Internal Audit and QA Dept that in order to minimise the risk of customer fraud only tele-sales order team personnel should have access to maintaining the delivery address. This is a company standard adopted in line with the Mail Order Fraud Prevention Scheme sponsored by the UK Government.

Draw the process model for the way the amendments to the existing process should work. (16 marks)
You do not need to show external pools.
You must show swimlanes for who is performing which processes.

If you want a review of your answers by a Business Analyst please complete the question and email your answer to ISEBRE@smart-BA.com. There is a charge for this service - please pay online at http://www.smart-ba.com/purchase

ISEB Syllabus Section 6 exam style revision question – data model

For the following data model, list 5 business requirements that are expressed in the following data model:

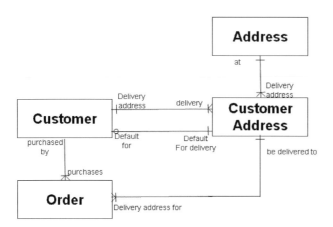

If you want a review of your answers by a Business Analyst please complete the question and email your answer to ISEBRE@smart-BA.com. There is a charge for this service - please pay online at http://www.smart-ba.com/purchase

ISEB Syllabus Section 6 exam style revision question – process model MODEL ANSWER

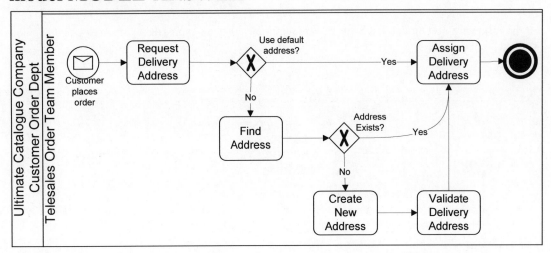

Valid alternative:

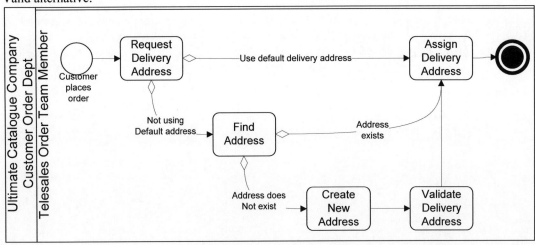

Elements from both diagrams can be combined.

©Guy Beauchamp 2009

Questions? ISEBRE@smart-BA.com

ISEB Syllabus Section 6 exam style revision question – data model MODEL ANSWER

A Customer must purchase 1 or more Orders.

An Order must be purchased by one Customer.

A Customer must have one default for delivery Customer Address

A Customer Address may be the default delivery address for zero or 1 Customer.

A Customer must have 1 or more delivery Customer Addresses.

A Customer Address must be the delivery address for 1 Customer.

A Customer Address must be the delivery address for 1 or more Orders.

An Order must be delivered to 1 Customer Address.

A Customer Address must be at 1 Address

An Address must be the delivery address for 1 or more Customer Addresses.

Notes:
1. Any 5 of the above will do.
2. Do not bother doing more than 5: the examiner will mark the first 5 and ignore the rest. If you do not want an examiner to mark an answer, clearly strike it through.

ISEB Syllabus Section 7: Documenting the Requirements

Key points:

Requirements need to be managed and this is looked at in more detail in ISEB Syllabus Section 10 Requirements Management. This section will consider what needs to be documented about requirements in order that they can be managed.

The basic concept is that of a catalogue of requirements that – taken together – fully define the change requirements for a project.

The following table shows **when** the requirements catalogue would be used and **what for**.

Phase	Use
Identify change	• Scope the high level requirements of the project
Analyse requirements	• Document the products of requirements analysis
Specify solution	• Check that the solution being designed incorporates all the requirements and no more • Mediation of any compromises to the requirements due to design constraints
Develop solution	• Check that every requirement that has been designed in to the solution is developed • Check that no extra requirements are being added in
Test solution	• The requirements acceptance criteria form the basis of user acceptance test cases and scripts • Prove that all requirements designed in to the solution are being delivered
Rollout solution	• Development of user procedures • Development of user training • Development of cutover activities (to manage the interim period while change is being made)
Monitor solution	• Check that all monitoring incorporates the requirements and no more

You have already understand about types of requirement and their hierarchy covered in ISEB Syllabus Section 3 Hierarchy of Requirements.

This section will introduce the information you need to capture about the requirements themselves and this breaks down in to the following components:

Requirements Catalogue
- Identifier
- Description
- Requirement type

- Acceptance criteria
- Source/Owner
- Rationale/Benefits
- Non-functional requirements
- Priority
- Related requirements/documents
- Version control/status
- History of changes

Each component is described in detail in the following section.

Note: the style, terminology and format that different organisations use to catalogue requirements will vary considerably, but they will almost always cover the components listed above and sometimes more.

Questions? ISEBRE@smart-BA.com

Detail:

Section	Description
Identifier	Unique identifier to distinguish requirements
Description	The requirement itself. This is a bit of a 'grey' area as process models and data models are detailed requirements but you would not expect to see a catalogue entry for each one of those. What you would expect here is any requirement that can be written in sentence form.
Requirement type	Refer to ISEB Syllabus Section 3 Hierarchy of Requirements for details. The valid types you would see in the catalogue are • general • business • functional • non-functional • detailed rule
Acceptance criteria	The test(s) that the business agree would define that the requirement has been delivered.
Source/Owner	Who was involved in the generation of the requirement.
Rationale/Benefits	What project objectives the requirement contributes to achieving.
Priority	Defines if the requirement is • Must have • Should have • Could have • Won't have/Wish list/Would have next time Requirements prioritisation is covered in more detail in ISEB Syllabus Section 8 Requirements Analysis
Related requirements/documents	Any references to documents that will aid in the understanding the requirement (such as Project Terms of Reference or Project Initiation Document)
Version control/status	Largely dependant on organisation standards but typically the requirement will be in a status of • proposed • signed off • rejected
History of changes	Who has changed what, when and why.

Example catalogue entry:

Section	Example
Identifier	65
Description	The system should prompt the user to confirm the delivery address with the customer when an order is placed.
Requirement type	High level functional requirement
Acceptance criteria	1. When payment has been taken a prompt is displayed to the user for the delivery address and the system should be ready to accept the address. 2. When the customer account is charged a prompt is displayed to the user for the delivery address and the system should be ready to accept the address.
Source/Owner	Ms C. Gray - telesales order process subject matter expert Mr E. Clarke - a tele-sales order team member Ms. D. Bartlett - Project Manager Ms. F. Harrison - Business Analyst
Rationale/Benefits	Reduce the percentage of orders returned due incorrect delivery address by 66%.
Priority	Must have.
Related requirements/documents	Order Delivery Address Project Terms of Reference (v1.0)
Version control/status	Proposed 2/2/2020
History of changes	Ms. F. Harrison created the requirement 2/2/2020 Ms E.Clarke updated acceptance criteria 3/2/2020

Questions? ISEBRE@smart-BA.com

Further Reading for Syllabus Section 7

Business Analysis – Debra Paul and Donald Yeates
Published by: The British Computer Society
ISBN 1-902505-70-0
Price: £20.00 from BCS and Amazon etc
Relevant Chapters/sections:
Chapter 9 section Documenting The Requirements P 149

Requirements Engineering by Gerald Kotonya and Ian Sommerville
Published by: John Willey & Sons
ISBN: 0-471-97208-8
Price: £36.00 from Amazon etc
Relevant Chapters/sections:
Chapter 5 – Requirements Management section 5.2 Requirements Identification and Storage p 117-123

For a more general analysis of documenting requirements see
Business Analysis Body of Knowledge (BABOK) v1.6 from the International Institute of Business Analysts
(IIBA) http://www.theiiba.org/AM/Template.cfm?Section=Body_of_Knowledge – free
Relevant Chapters/sections:
5.9 Task: Document Requirements p 205-207

Questions? ISEBRE@smart-BA.com

ISEB Certificate in Requirements Engineering
Self Study 'JEEP' Manual

ISEB Syllabus Section 7 exam style revision question

Mr A. Smith, Director of Customer Order Delivery Division at Ultimate Catalogue Company has initiated a project which has an objective to reduce the percentage of orders returned due incorrect delivery address by 66%.

For the Business and Functional requirements you documented in the answer to ISEB Syllabus Section 3, complete the following requirements catalogue partial entries.
(Note: it is very common for ISEB exam papers to refer you back to answers you gave to earlier questions. Be sure that you do just that and explicitly reference or copy the answer you previously gave).

Business Requirement:

Section	
Identifier	
Description	
Requirement type	
Acceptance criteria	
Rationale/Benefits	

Functional Requirement:

Section	
Identifier	
Description	
Requirement type	
Acceptance criteria	
Rationale/Benefits	

If you want a review of your answers by a Business Analyst please complete the question and email your answer to ISEBRE@smart-BA.com. There is a charge for this service - please pay online at http://www.smart-ba.com/purchase

ISEB Syllabus Section 7 exam style revision question MODEL ANSWER

Business Requirement:

Section		Notes
Identifier	01	Any number will do.
Description	Be able to validate a delivery address.	Your requirement goes here.
Acceptance criteria	Solution will not allow the user to progress with an invalid address.	Any reasonable acceptance criteria will do. Note the acceptance test refers to the solution and not the system.
Rationale/Benefits	Contributes to the objective "reduce the percentage of orders returned due incorrect delivery address by 66%."	

Functional Requirement:

Section		Notes
Identifier	02	Any number except for the number used above will do.
Description	The system will validate a delivery address.	Your requirement goes here.
Acceptance criteria	System will not allow the user to progress with an invalid address.	Any reasonable acceptance criteria will do. Note the acceptance test refers to the system and not the solution.
Rationale/Benefits	Contributes to the objective "reduce the percentage of orders returned due incorrect delivery address by 66%."	

ISEB Syllabus Section 8: Requirements Analysis

Key points:

Requirements need to be
1. prioritised
2. analysed for errors

1. **Requirements Prioritisation**
   The following types of requirement prioritisation (know as MoSCoW) should suffice for the ISEB exam:

Priority	Description
Must have	Without this requirement the project cannot achieve it's objectives and will therefore be classed as a failure. "MUST" is also sometimes known as an acronym for the **M**inimum **U**sable **S**ub**S**e**T** of requirements.
Should have	Without this requirement, the project can still achieve its objectives, but not as well. It will be successful but it could have been more successful with this requirement.
Could have	Can be thought of as 'nice to have' requirements: having or not having this objective will not impact on the assessment of whether the project was successful (whether it achieved its objectives) but it would be good if the project could implement the requirement.
Won't have	Also known as 'Wish list' or 'Would have next time'. The requirement has so little value to the project it is not even a 'could have'. In effect requirements with this priority are out of project scope.

2. **Analysing requirements for errors**
   Requirements need to be analysed to check for errors in them. The common errors are listed in this table:

Error type	Description	Solutions
Congruence	A requirement that does not contribute to achieving any project objectives.	1. prioritise the requirement as Could or Won't have or 2. define an objective it does contribute to or 3. rework the requirement to contribute to an existing objective
Overlapping requirements	Requirements that – in part – deal with the same change.	1. rework the requirements
Conflicting requirements	2 requirements that specify opposite changes.	1. rework the requirements
Ambiguity	The requirement can be interpreted in many different ways.	1. rework the requirement or 2. use a glossary to define terms
Requirements realism/feasibility	The requirement may be valid in terms of project objectives, but	1. rework requirement or 2. rework objectives and then

Error type	Description	Solutions
	subject matter experts know it is not feasible.	rework requirement
Requirements testability	There is no (reasonable) way of testing whether the requirement has been satisfied or not.	1. rework requirement

©Guy Beauchamp 2009

Questions? ISEBRE@smart-BA.com

Detail:

1. Requirements Prioritisation

Remember: Objectives are measures that can increased, decreased or maintained and if they hit a certain target value equate to project success.

Requirements are changes required in order to achieve project objectives.

Given the above statements it follows that if there is a requirement that – if excluded – means the project cannot achieve its objectives then it **must** have that requirement. If that requirement is dropped then the project has already failed and it might as well stop there and then.

Example: If the objective of the Customer Delivery Address project is "to reduce the percentage of orders returned due incorrect delivery address by 66%".

Functional requirement: "The system should prompt the user to confirm the delivery address with the customer when an order is placed."

- The question about whether this is a 'must have' requirement then becomes "can the project reduce the percentage of orders returned due incorrect delivery address by 66% if the system can not prompt the user to confirm the delivery address with the customer when an order is placed"?
- If the answer is "The system must be able to prompt he user to confirm the delivery address with the customer when an order is placed *so that the system will* reduce the percentage of orders returned due incorrect delivery address by 66%" then the requirement is a 'must have'.
- If the answer is "There are other ways to reduce the percentage of orders returned due incorrect delivery address by 66%" then the question is now whether that requirement is a "should have".
- In order to work out if it should be a 'should have' requirement the question must be asked "will the requirement to prompt the user to confirm the delivery address with the customer when an order is placed enable the project to achieve its objectives better with it than without it?"
- If the answer is "yes, the project will reduce the percentage of orders returned due incorrect delivery address by 75%" then the requirement is a 'should have'.
- If the answer is "no, it won't make any difference to how well the project achieves it objectives" then the question becomes is the requirement a "could have".
- In order to work out if this is a 'could have requirement' an **arbitrary** decision has to be taken about whether "it would be *good* if the project could implement the requirement". The stakeholders who make the go/no go decision on requirements sign off should make this decision.
- If it is not accepted as being "*good*" for the project to implement this requirement then it becomes a "Won't have" requirement.

Questions? ISEBRE@smart-BA.com

2. Analysing requirements for errors

Remember: Objectives are measures that can increased, decreased or maintained and if they hit a certain target value equate to project success.

Example: The objective of the Customer Delivery Address project is "to reduce the percentage of orders returned due incorrect delivery address by 66%".

Error type	Description	Example requirement that has the error
Congruence	A requirement that does not contribute to achieving any project objectives.	The system must allow for goods being returned to be picked up from a different address to where they were delivered.
Overlapping requirements	Requirements that – in part – deal with the same change.	1st requirement: The system should prompt the user to confirm the delivery address with the customer when an order is placed. 2nd requirement: The system must ensure that the user validates the delivery address with the customer.
Conflicting requirements	2 requirements that specify opposite changes.	1st requirement: for all orders the delivery address should default to the default delivery address for the customer. 2nd requirement: for all orders the delivery address should initially be blank (to force the sales rep to actively select one).
Ambiguity	The requirement can be interpreted in many different ways.	Requirement: The system should allow users to associate any address with a customer. - "associate" is ambiguous and can be interpreted in many ways.
Requirements realism/feasibility	The requirement may be valid in terms of project objectives, but subject matter experts know it is not feasible.	The system should allow the user to access a real time satellite view of the UK to validate an address. - it can be argued this will help the project achieve its objectives it is just highly unlikely to be feasible for a catalogue company!
Requirements testability	There is no (reasonable) way of testing whether the requirement has been satisfied or not.	The system should be intuitive. - what tests would be run that would 'prove' the solution is intuitive? The term 'intuitive' in this context is also ambiguous.

And finally – do not think this is an exhaustive list of errors. You must be able to demonstrate to your satisfaction that a requirement is fit for purpose before it can be considered as such.

Questions? ISEBRE@smart-BA.com

Further Reading for Syllabus Section 8

This document: ISEB Syllabus Section 2: Nature and problems of Requirements! There is a large overlap between that ISEB Syllabus Section and this one. The reading list for that section applies here as well and is reproduced for convenience:

Business Analysis – Debra Paul and Donald Yeates
Published by: The British Computer Society
ISBN 1-902505-70-0
Price: £20.00 from BCS and Amazon etc
Relevant Chapters/sections:
Chapter 9 – Requirements Engineering
        section The Problems With Requirements pages135-137 and
        section Requirements Analysis
        pages 147-149

Requirements Engineering by Gerald Kotonya and Ian Sommerville
Published by: John Willey & Sons
ISBN: 0-471-97208-8
Price: £36.00 from Amazon etc
Relevant Chapters/sections:
Chapter 4 – Requirements Validation 4.1.3 Requirements Checklists p 95-100

For a more general analysis of validating requirements see
Business Analysis Body of Knowledge (BABOK) v1.6 from the International Institute of Business Analysts (IIBA) http://www.theiiba.org/AM/Template.cfm?Section=Body_of_Knowledge – free
Relevant Chapters/sections:
5.11 Task: Verify Requirements P208-211

ISEB Certificate in Requirements Engineering

Self Study 'JEEP' Manual

ISEB Syllabus Section 8 exam style revision question

Mr A. Smith, Director of Customer Order Delivery Division at Ultimate Catalogue Company has initiated a project which has an objective to reduce the percentage of orders returned due incorrect delivery address by 66%.

Prioritise the following requirements.

If you want a review of your answers by a Business Analyst please complete the question and email your answer to ISEBRE@smart-BA.com. There is a charge for this service - please pay online at http://www.smart-ba.com/purchase

Requirement Type	Requirement	Priority	Justification
Business requirement	The solution should set the customer's default delivery address for their first order to their billing address.		
Functional requirement	The system will validate the customer's billing address.		
Non-Functional requirement	The system will be able to validate up to 2,500 delivery addresses per day.		
Technical requirement	Postcodes must be validated by checking they exist on the Post Office Address File.		
Data requirement	It must be possible to hold special delivery instructions against customer delivery addresses.		
Detailed requirement	The name of the telesales order team member who recorded a delivery address must recorded for each delivery address for a customer.		

©Guy Beauchamp 2009

ISEB Syllabus Section 8 exam style revision question MODEL ANSWER

Requirement Type	Requirement	Priority	Justification
Business requirement	The solution should set the customer's default delivery address for their first order to their billing address.	Could	It won't directly help achieve the objective but it would be a good thing.
Functional requirement	The system will validate the customer's billing address.	Won't	This does not contribute to achieving project objectives.
Non-Functional requirement	The system will be able to validate up to 2,500 delivery addresses per day.	Must	This is the number of deliveries made a day and if the system cannot support that volume it cannot achieve project objectives.
Technical requirement	Postcodes must be validated by checking they exist on the Post Office Address File.	Must	The solution cannot achieve objectives without validating postcodes and there are technical requirements about how to do that.
Data requirement	It must be possible to hold special delivery instructions against customer delivery addresses.	Should	The project is seeking to solve the problem of failed deliveries due to poor addresses, but this would help the delivery drivers and so would help make sure even more deliveries were successfully made.
Detailed requirement	The name of the telesales order team member who recorded a delivery address must recorded for each delivery address for a customer.	Won't	Does not contribute to project objective or help in any obvious way.

ISEB Syllabus Section 9: Requirements Validation

Key points:

Requirements need to be validated through
1. Prototyping
2. Reviews
3. Sign-off of requirements document

1. Prototyping

Prototyping is concerned with mocking-up a user/solution interface so that users can see how it is envisaged the solution will work. This takes the requirements out of the abstracted, analytical way of identifying and documenting them and presents them as the users would interact with the solution that has delivered them.

Two objectives for prototyping:
1. confirm the requirements have been understood correctly so far
2. eliciting new requirements (usually of the tacit and semi-tacit kind because it is not until the solution is seen that it suddenly becomes obvious the Business Analyst didn't know something the users were taking as read)

2. Reviews

This refers to reviews with others, not the Business Analyst checking the requirements they have documented. Reviews can be formal or not and structured or not. We will look at a couple of techniques:

- subject matter expert reviews – suitable for individuals who know about the area being analysed and usually have been involved in the elicitation process review the analysis products
- workshop reviews – suitable where more than 1 person knows about the area being analysed and usually have been involved in the elicitation process review the analysis products
- structured walkthroughs – suitable for ensuring the quality and content of the analysis products and to be regarded as the last chance before sign-off to identify any changes required to analysis products

3. Sign-off of requirements

The content of the sign-off document will be the definitive statement of the change requirements that are to have a solution designed for them.

The purpose of the document is to formally state that solution design work can now commence so any changes to the requirements from here on in need to be managed and controlled in order to be able to maintain control over the rest of the solution development life cycle.

smart·BA
distance learning programme

Detail

1. Prototyping

Prototyping is concerned with mocking-up a user/solution interface so that users can see how it is envisaged the solution will work. This takes the requirements out of the abstracted, analytical way of identifying and documenting them and presents them as the users would interact with the solution that has delivered them.

Two objectives for prototyping:

1. confirm the requirements have been understood correctly so far
2. eliciting new requirements (usually of the tacit and semi-tacit kind because it is not until the solution is seen that it suddenly becomes obvious the Business Analyst didn't know something the users were taking as read)

There are a range of prototypes than can be developed from a paper based mock-up of one particular user function to functionally working computerised whole solution.

Prototype dimension	Lowest	Highest
Scope	One user function One location One user	All user functions All locations All users (in theory, never in practice)
Functionality	No functionality – typically paper or picture based *and annotated as required* No data created or updated	Fully user interactive functionality Data created and updated by the functions Typically computerised system functionality using tools such as Access.
Fidelity	**No** (intentional) aspects of the look and feel of the delivered solution in terms of • screen organisation and hierarchy • screen fields layout • screen colour and fonts • adherence to application standards • report layout and standards	**All** aspects of the look and feel of the delivered solution in terms of • screen organisation and hierarchy • screen fields layout • screen colour and fonts • adherence to application standards • report layout and standards

The trade off is this:

The lower the scope, functionality and fidelity, the less likely that so-far hidden tacit and semi-tacit requirements will be discovered.

The higher the scope, functionality and fidelity, the longer and more costly it is to develop the prototype and the greater the risk that users will see it as the full solution, so they see no further work required and may be reluctant to let the prototype go!

2. Reviews

- **subject matter expert reviews** – suitable for individuals who know about the area being analysed and usually have been involved in the elicitation process review the analysis products.
  The requirements are prepared to a point where the Business Analyst needs confirmation that they are correct so far. A good technique (but not the only one) for this stage is Use Case scenario modelling. This can be used in conjunction with (but not as a replacement for) the review of the documentation of your requirements as covered in previous sections.

Use Case is part of Unified Modelling Language (UML). One Use Case is equivalent to one top level process step and they are both named as Verb+Noun. E.g. "Record Delivery Address". The Use Case always shows the Actor's intent in using the Use Case – an Actor is a person or system who interacts with the solution. The following is the Use Case diagram for "Record Delivery Address":

Notes:
- The arrows on the lines between Actors and Use Cases are optional and show initiation, not process flow. ***This is not a process model.***
- The symbol for an actor which is a system or application is:

The Use Case is documented using Scenarios.
A Scenario is set of circumstances under which a Use Case is used.
It has a structure of:

- **Pre-conditions** – what must be true before this Use Case can begin. Example: A "Telesales Order Team Member" must be logged on to the solution and an order has just been placed by a "Customer".
- **Post-conditions** – what is true after the Use Case has finished. Example: A delivery address has been defined for the "Customer" order or the order is marked for cancellation.
- There are 2 ways of documenting the Scenario – that is documenting what Actor and Solution interactions take place in order to achieve the Actor's intent of "Record Delivery Address".

Whole Solution Format – the scenario is presented from the perspective of how the solution will work for **all** scenarios – example: start with the route through the use case that is the most common route, this also known as the Happy Day or Standard route:

Questions? ISEBRE@smart-BA.com

1. The Solution displays a list of known "Customer" delivery addresses with the default delivery address already selected and prompts the "Telesales Order Team Member" to ask the "Customer" if they want to use their default delivery address.
2. The "Telesales Order Team Member" records that the "Customer" does want to use the default delivery address.
3. The Solution associates the default delivery address with customer order and prompts the "Telesales Order Team Member" to confirm.
4. The "Telesales Order Team Member" confirms.

- Then list the Alternatives – for *each* interaction between "Telesales Order Team Member" and "Customer" and Solution this section records what might happen instead but is still a normal transaction (nothing has 'gone wrong') presenting the Alternative scenario and the alternative interactions that take place in order to achieve the Actor's intent of "Record Delivery Address". Example of an Alternative for statement 2 in the scenario:

  2a. (in the case that) The "Customer" wants to use an existing alternative delivery address

  > 2a1. The "Telesales Order Team Member" selects a "Customer" delivery address that is not the default.
  > 2a2. Go back to step 3.

- Then list the Exceptions – for each interaction between "Telesales Order Team Member" and "Customer" and Solution this section records what might happen instead and is **not** still a normal transaction (something has 'gone wrong') presenting the Exception scenario and the interactions that take place in order to achieve the Actor's intent of "Record Delivery Address". Example Exception for statement 2 in the scenario:

  2a. (in the case that) The "Customer" wants to use a new delivery address that Ultimate Catalogue Company does not deliver to (e.g. oversees)

  > 2a1. The "Telesales Order Team Member" advises that the order can only be delivered to UK addresses.
  > 2a2. The "Customer" advises they wish to cancel the order.
  > 2a3. The Solution marks the "Customer" order as "cancel pending"
  > 2a4. Exit this Use Case *(to allow the "Telesales Order Team Member" to initiate the "Cancel Order" Use Case)*

An alternative to the Whole Solution Scenario Format is **Business Scenario Format** – the documentation is presented from the perspective of how the solution will work for **each** scenario in turn.

First the scenarios are listed out and numbered:

1. "Customer" orders goods to be delivered to default delivery address.
2. "Customer" orders goods to be delivered to an existing non-default delivery address.
3. "Customer" orders goods to be delivered to an address that Ultimate Catalogue Company does not deliver to.

Then each scenario is documented:

1. "Customer" orders goods to be delivered to default delivery address.

1.1. The Solution displays a list of known "Customer" delivery addresses with the default delivery address already selected and prompts the "Telesales Order Team Member" to ask the "Customer" if they want to use their default delivery address.

1.2 The "Telesales Order Team Member" records that the "Customer" does want to use the default delivery address.

1.3 The Solution associates the default delivery address with customer order and prompts the "Telesales Order Team Member" to confirm.

1.4 The "Telesales Order Team Member" confirms.

2. "Customer" orders goods to be delivered to an existing non-default delivery address.

2.1. The Solution displays a list of known "Customer" delivery addresses with the default delivery address already selected and prompts the "Telesales Order Team Member" to ask the "Customer" if they want to use their default delivery address.

2.2 The "Telesales Order Team Member" selects a "Customer" delivery address that is not the default.

3.3 The Solution associates the default delivery address with customer order and prompts the "Telesales Order Team Member" to confirm.

4.4 The "Telesales Order Team Member" confirms.

3. "Customer" orders goods to be delivered to an existing non-default delivery address.

3.1. The Solution displays a list of known "Customer" delivery addresses with the default delivery address already selected and prompts the "Telesales Order Team Member" to ask the "Customer" if they want to use their default delivery address.

3.2. The "Customer" requests goods to be delivered to an address (that Ultimate Catalogue Company does not deliver to).

3.2. The "Telesales Order Team Member" advises that the order can only be delivered to UK addresses.

3.3. The "Customer" advises they wish to cancel the order.

3.4. The Solution marks the "Customer" order as "cancel pending"

Note that even these scenarios can have Alternatives and Exceptions documented for them just as for the Whole Solution Scenario Format.

Which is the better scenario format?

It depends on what you want to do and who you have available to do it: If you want the whole solution reviewed and you have a subject matter expert for the whole solution then use the whole solution scenario format. If, on the other hand, you want a review of a particular area (perhaps because of complexity) and you have an expert in that area, use the business scenario format. You can generate scenarios in both formats for different audiences if needs be.

There is a lot more to UML (out of scope for the exam) and Use Case diagrams (also out of scope) – if you want to find out more then sources are listed in the Further Reading section at the end of this section.

- **workshop reviews** – suitable where more than 1 person knows about the area being analysed and usually have been involved in the elicitation process review the analysis products

Essentially the same as individual reviews (with the exception of the structured walkthrough – see next section).

Analyse who needs to attend and what their remit is (what are they entitled to comment on and make decisions about).

Conduct the workshop as per an interview (see ISEB Syllabus Section 5 Requirements Elicitation in this manual) – the objective of the workshop is to review the requirements.

- **structured walkthroughs** – suitable for ensuring the quality and content of the analysis products and to be regarded as the last chance before sign-off to identify any changes required to analysis products.

  Structured Walkthroughs are a workshop where the roles, structure and format have been defined:

Roles:

Role	Responsibility
Chairman	**Before the walkthrough:** Announces walkthrough – co-ordinates logistics Invites attendees Issues material for review to Expert Reviewers Issues list of questions and queries generated by Expert Reviewers **At the walkthrough:** Controls start of walkthrough – introduces it Maintains control during the walkthrough Calls for a walkthrough decision • accept product as is • accept product with no further review if agreed changes are made after the walkthrough • rejects product – another walkthrough will be required Closes the walkthrough
Expert Reviewers	Anyone who has a vested interest in making sure the analysis products are correct and fit for purpose so could include: • Business Analysts • Project Subject Matter Experts • Project Users • Project Manager • Project Designers and Programmers • Project Testers **Before the walkthrough** Receives the material to be reviewed Prepares and sends to Chairman a list of questions and queries for the walkthrough **At the walkthrough** At the relevant points in the walkthrough raises their questions and queries Makes an 'accept' or 'reject' decision on the response Makes the walkthrough decision at the end **After the walkthrough**

Role	Responsibility
	If any further work is required based on comments made by or knowledge held by an Expert Reviewer, they undertake it using the documentation from the Scribe with the relevant BAs.
Scribe	Ideally should be a BA and better still involved in the production of the product being reviewed. **Before the walkthrough** Constructs of joint list of issues and queries from the Expert Reviewers **At the walkthrough** Documents meeting (time, place, subject and participants) Records unresolved questions and queries Records walkthrough decision **After the walkthrough** Sends any unresolved questions and queries to the Presenter for further work
Presenter	Should be a BA heavily involved if not the author of the product being reviewed. **Before the walkthrough** Requests walkthrough Supplies material for review Reviews questions and queries that the expert reviewers raise **At the walkthrough** Presents the material for review Answers the questions and queries as they are raised **After the walkthrough** If any further work is required, undertakes it using the documentation from the Scribe involving any Expert Reviewers as needed.

Structure

The walkthrough has a prescribed structure:

a. Chairman opens the meeting
b. Presenter starts to present product
c. Expert reviewers raises questions and queries at the appropriate point
d. Presenter answers question or query
e. Expert Reviewer accepts or rejects answer (steps c, d and e are the 'challenge, response, decision' cycle)
f. Rejected answers are recorded by the Scribe so that they can be progressed by the Presenter and Expert Reviewer after the meeting.
g. When the product has been presented and all questions and queries raised the Chairman closes the meeting

Notes:

1. There are no 'passive' roles in the walkthrough.
2. Everyone should stick to the remit of their role.
3. The Chairman must stop dead any 'lets try to fix it' conversations by Presenter and/or Expert Reviewers.
4. The Chairman must stop dead any criticism of the Presenter (it is the product being reviewed, not the Presenter).

Questions? ISEBRE@smart-BA.com

5. The Chairman must watch out for and curtail any protectionism by the Presenter for their Product.
6. The Expert Reviewers should be those who know about the product being reviewed and the subject area: they should be Experts and some are likely to be people who will be using the analysis products (such as solutions designers).
7. The Scribe must document all unresolved questions and queries thoroughly: what is queried, why, who by.
8. The Presenter should be glad if any errors are detected: the walkthrough did not create them, just uncovered them and if they had not been uncovered but left until testing or implementation the consequences in terms of time and money would be far worse.

3. Sign-off of requirements
The content of the sign-off document will be the definitive statement of the change requirements that are to have a solution designed for them.

The purpose of the document is to formally state that solution design work can now commence so any changes to the requirements from here on in need to be managed and controlled in order to be able to maintain control over the rest of the solution development life cycle.

The content of Requirements documentation has been covered in ISEB Syllabus Section 7 – Documenting The Requirements.

Sign-off must be
- Auditable: either physically or some other way it must be possible to demonstrate that all signatories have agreed the deliverables are complete.
- By the right people: all stakeholders who are authorised by the organisation to accept or reject the deliverables must sign-off the deliverables.

smart·BA
distance learning programme

Further Reading for Syllabus Section 9

This document: ISEB Syllabus Section 2: Nature and problems of Requirements! There is a large overlap between that ISEB Syllabus Section and this one. The reading list for that section applies here as well and is reproduced for convenience:

Business Analysis – Debra Paul and Donald Yeates
Published by: The British Computer Society
ISBN 1-902505-70-0
Price: £20.00 from BCS and Amazon etc
Relevant Chapters/sections:
Chapter 9 – Requirements Engineering
        section Validating Requirements page 155
Chapter 5 – Investigation Techniques
        section Prototyping pages 77-78
Chapter 10 – Modelling the IT System
        Section Modelling Systems Functions pages 159-163

Requirements Engineering by Gerald Kotonya and Ian Sommerville
Published by: John Willey & Sons
ISBN: 0-471-97208-8
Price: £36.00 from Amazon etc
Relevant Chapters/sections:
Chapter 4 – Requirements Validation 4.2 Prototyping p 100-103

Questions? ISEBRE@smart-BA.com

ISEB Syllabus Section 9 exam style revision question

There is a process to set the default delivery address for a customer. When a telesales order team member is taking an order for a new customer, they record the delivery address and make this the default delivery address for that customer.

The process should be for the telesales order team member to capture the customer's house number or name and postcode. The solution should then look up the full address and display it to the telesales order team member who confirms it with customer. If elements of the address (except house name/number and postcode) need changing, the telesales order team member should be able to make them, or they can enter a new house no/name postcode combination for lookup. In exceptional circumstances the telesales order team member may need to create an address that cannot be validated – the system should allow the user to do this but require them to annotate the delivery address with the reason why this address has been created and automatically attach their user identification for audit purposes.

When an address has been selected the system needs to associate it with the customer as the default delivery address.

1. Define a Use Case for "set default delivery address", draw a use case diagram and document the scenarios in the format of your choice. (12 marks)
2. Sketch out a prototype for the screen(s) that support this process.

If you want a review of your answers by a Business Analyst please complete the question and email your answer to ISEBRE@smart-BA.com. There is a charge for this service - please pay online at http://www.smart-ba.com/purchase

ISEB Syllabus Section 9 exam style revision question MODEL ANSWER

1. Define a Use Case for "set default delivery address", draw a use case diagram and document the scenarios in the format of your choice. (12 marks)

Pre-conditions:
- A "Telesales Order Team Member" is logged on to the solution.
- A "Customer" has placed an order.

Post-conditions:
- a default delivery address exists for the customer

Whole Solution format:
1. The solution prompts the "Telesales Order Team Member" to capture the "Customer's" house number or name and postcode.
2. The "Telesales Order Team Member" enters the "Customer's" house number or name and postcode.
3. The solution displays the full address and prompts for confirmation.
4. The "Telesales Order Team Member" confirms the address with the "Customer".
5. The solution associates the address with the "Customer" as the default delivery address.

Alternatives:
4a. The "Customer" advises some elements (not house number/name or postcode) of the address need changing
    4a.1 The "Telesales Order Team Member" changes the elements that need changing.
    4a.2 Return to 4.
4b. The "Customer" advises that the house number/name and/or postcode need changing
    4b.1 Return to 2.
Extensions:
3a. The solution cannot find the house number/name and postcode combination.
    3a.1 The "Telesales Order Team Member" enters the full delivery address and any optional explanatory comments.
    3a.2 The solution adds the audit information to the address.

3a.3 Return to 4.

Business Scenario Format
1. The "Customer" has a standard delivery address with no changes required.
2. The "Customer" has a standard delivery address with changes required but not to house name/number or postcode.
3. The "Customer" has a standard delivery address with changes required to house name/number and/or postcode.
4. The solution cannot find the address the "Customer" supplies.

1. The "Customer" has a standard delivery address with no changes required.
   a. The solution prompts the "Telesales Order Team Member" to capture the "Customer's" house number or name and postcode.
   b. The "Telesales Order Team Member" enters the "Customer's" house number or name and postcode.
   c. The solution displays the full address and prompts for confirmation.
   d. The "Telesales Order Team Member" confirms the address with the "Customer".
   e. The solution associates the address with the "Customer" as the default delivery address.

2. The "Customer" has a standard delivery address with changes required but not to house name/number or postcode.
   a. The solution prompts the "Telesales Order Team Member" to capture the "Customer's" house number or name and postcode.
   b. The "Telesales Order Team Member" enters the "Customer's" house number or name and postcode.
   c. The solution displays the full address and prompts for confirmation.
   d. The "Customer" advises changes required but not to house name/number.
   e. The "Telesales Order Team Member" changes the elements that need changing.
   f. The "Telesales Order Team Member" confirms the address with the "Customer".
   g. The solution associates the address with the "Customer" as the default delivery address.

3. The "Customer" has a standard delivery address with changes required to house name/number and/or postcode.
   a. The solution prompts the "Telesales Order Team Member" to capture the "Customer's" house number or name and postcode.
   b. The "Telesales Order Team Member" enters the "Customer's" house number or name and postcode.
   c. The solution displays the full address and prompts for confirmation.
   d. The "Telesales Order Team Member" changes the house name/number and/or postcode
   e. Return to start of relevant scenario.

4. The solution cannot find the address the "Customer" supplies.
   a. The solution prompts the "Telesales Order Team Member" to capture the "Customer's" house number or name and postcode.
   b. The "Telesales Order Team Member" enters the "Customer's" house number or name and postcode.

   c.   The solution advises it cannot display the full address.

   d.   The "Telesales Order Team Member" enters an address and optionally any explanatory comments.

   e.   The solution adds audit information to the address.

   f.   The "Telesales Order Team Member" confirms the address with the "Customer".

   g.   The solution associates the address with the "Customer" as the default delivery address.

Notes

1. Business Scenario format inevitably means writing out more as you will be repeating steps for each scenario. Given the choice document as whole solution format as it is quicker to write down.

2. You can use any terminology that communicates how the scenario proceeds: this example uses "return to" but you can use "go to" or any other phrase that communicate the flow of the scenario.

3. Notice in Business Scenario Format for Scenario 3 The "Customer" has a standard delivery address with changes required to house name/number and/or postcode that the last statement is "Return to start of relevant scenario". This is because having entered a new house name/number and/or postcode we are effectively starting from the top as the new scenario that results could be any one of

   - The "Customer" has a standard delivery address with no changes required.
   - The "Customer" has a standard delivery address with changes required but not to house name/number or postcode.
   - The "Customer" has a standard delivery address with changes required to house name/number and/or postcode.
   - The solution cannot find the address the "Customer" supplies.

4. **You must model what has been asked for and not what you think might be needed.** For example, you might want build in that the address is valid but not one that the company delivers to. *This was not outlined in the question as needing to be modelled and so you should not model it!* Remember to answer the question, the whole question and nothing but the question.

Questions? ISEBRE@smart-BA.com

2. Sketch out a prototype for the screen(s) that support this process.

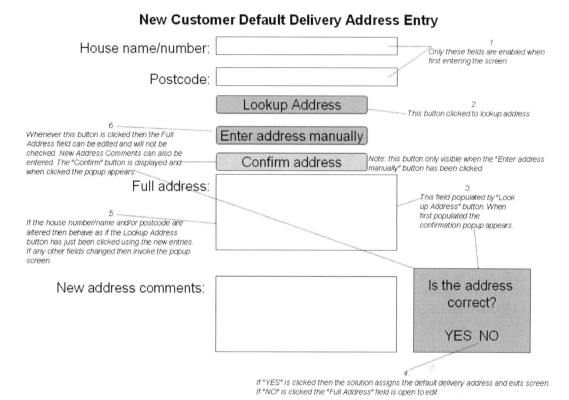

New Customer Default Delivery Address Entry

Notes:
1. Any sketch that can be followed without having someone there to explain it will be acceptable.
2. **You must model what has been asked for and not what you think might be needed.** For example, you might want build in that the address is valid but not one that the company delivers to. *This was not outlined in the question as needing to be modelled and so you should not model it!* Remember to answer the question, the whole question and nothing but the question.
3. You could draw multiple versions of the same screen to show the process if you want.

©Guy Beauchamp 2009
Questions? ISEBRE@smart-BA.com

ISEB Syllabus Section 10: Requirements Management

Key points:

Requirements need to be managed through the analysis and subsequent project phases.

1. **Stable and volatile requirements**

   Some requirements can be characterised as more likely to change than others – these are volatile requirements. The reasons for volatility include:
   - process requirements are more volatile than data requirements (business processes change more frequently than the data businesses use does)
   - changes in project personnel especially subject matter experts and other user representatives responsible for requirements sign-off
   - changes to the internal business environment (the business is taken over, or changes strategic direction and so on)
   - changes to the external business environment (changes to laws and regulations, economic factors, etc)
   - project scope changes
   - analysis has led to new understanding about what the business wants to achieve (changing the project objectives and or requirements)

2. **Management of change to requirements**

   There is a process to go through when managing changes to requirements:
   1. define the change
   2. analyse the benefits of the change
   3. prioritise the change
   4. analyse the cost to implement of the change
   5. analyse the impact of the change
   6. accept change
   7. schedule change
   8. implement change

   Note: at any point in the process the change may be rejected

3. **Traceability and ownership of requirements**

   In order to manage changes to requirements at any point in the Systems Development Life-Cycle (SDLC) there must be full backwards and forwards traceability of the requirement:
   - Who was involved in generating the requirement?
   - When was the requirement generated?
   - Who signed it off as a requirement?
   - When was it signed off?
   - What objectives does it contribute to achieving?
   - What processes does it impact?
   - What data areas does it impact?
   - What non-functional requirements does it impact?
   - What modules implement it?
   - What databases implement it?
   - What screens are impacted?

Questions? ISEBRE@smart-BA.com

- What reports are impacted?
- What other functionality is impacted?
- What tests prove its delivery?
- What migration and cutover activities will be impacted?
- What areas of the business will be impacted (organisation and location)?

4. **CASE (Computer Aided Software Engineering) tools for Requirements Engineering**
    - they are a centralised repository of requirements
    - there are CARE (Computer Aided Requirements Engineering) tools but these are being merged with CASE
    - the advantages are concerned with re-use and impact analysis benefits
    - the disadvantages are cost and how incorrect use makes a big mess very quickly!

Questions? ISEBRE@smart-BA.com

Detail.

1. **Stable and volatile requirements**
   Some requirements can be characterised as more likely to change than others – these are volatile requirements. The reasons for volatility include:
   - process requirements are more volatile than data requirements (business processes change more frequently than the data businesses use does)
     Ultimate Catalogue Company started out nearly 100 years ago when the owner set up a market stall selling items that were paid for in instalments. Each week he then went around his customers to collect payment. He had customers, he sold products and customers made payments. Today, Ultimate Catalogue Company has had 5 million customers who shop by phone and online, has multiple catalogues and no market stall, and payments are by direct debit and credit card. The processes to manage these changes have been significant, but the data has not changed as much: there are still customers, products, sales and payments. Process requirements are more likely to change than data requirements.
   - changes in project personnel especially subject matter experts and other user representatives responsible for requirements sign-off
     New people have new ideas, new drivers and objectives. In order to implement these new ideas etc they are likely to have new requirements and/or changes to the existing ones.
   - changes to the internal business environment (the business is taken over, or changes strategic direction and so on)
     Changes to the internal business environment can result in changes to objectives and therefore requirements. Even a change just in the organisation hierarchy can mean that the new project sponsor has different measures to apply that equate to success and so the requirements to achieve those new measures will change as well.
   - changes to the external business environment (changes to laws and regulations, economic factors, etc)
     The only constant in business is change. In order to be able to carry on conducting business, an organisation must adhere to all the relevant laws and regulations and maintain that compliance when the laws and regulations change. Competitors also force businesses to change as do market conditions (economic boom-bust cycles).
   - project scope changes
     The scope could be changing for reasons covered in the last three points, or it could be changing because when a project is running short or resource (be it time, money and/or people) then it can either increase resource and/or cut back on scope and/or quality. Scope changes can mean that those requirements or parts of requirements needed for the scope that has been cut need to change to reflect the new scope.
   - analysis has led to new understanding about what the business wants to achieve (changing the project objectives and or requirements)
     One of the most rewarding parts of Business Analysis is when users refine their thinking as they realise the consequences of what they are asking for as the result of analysis. For example, the objective "reduce the percentage of orders returned due incorrect delivery address by 66%" could be achieved by taking 66% fewer orders. Clearly this would not constitute success and leads to the realisation that there is an objective missing: "maintain

current order taking levels". This in turn leads to new non-functional requirements about the throughput of orders that must be supported and ease of use.

2. **Management of change to requirements**

    There is a process to go through when managing changes to requirements:

    1. Define the change.

        Using the same criteria covered in ISEB Syllabus Section 2 and 8, define what needs to change for which requirements

    2. Analyse the benefits of the change.

        What is the cost of not doing the change?

        Which objectives will the change to the requirements contribute to and can it be estimated how much?

    3. Prioritise the change.

        Using the criteria covered in ISEB Syllabus Section 8, assign a priority to the change.

    4. Analyse the cost to implement of the change.

        There will be System Development Life Cycle (SDLC) costs depending at what point in the SDLC the change is raised. Example, a change to a requirement at the end of analysis means going back to rework that requirement and then take the changes through to design. A change to requirements at the user acceptance stage means reworking that requirement, changing the design of the solution, the screens, codes and database schemas that were created to support it, changing the unit, link, system and user acceptance test scripts and performing those tests. There will also be business costs during the later stages of the SDLC: the business will have been preparing for the new solution (hiring and firing people, training users, restructuring, communicating with customers if needed and so on). The changed requirement could impact what the business has already done and there will be a cost to that as well.

    5. Analyse the impact of the change.

        Which process, data areas and associated non-functional requirements will be impacted?

        Which organisation units will be impacted? How?

        Is there any impact on locations?

        For applications that are being developed or integrate with the solution, what will be the impact?

        Will there need to be changes to supporting technology such as networks, telephones and so on?

        Which business customers (if any) will be impacted?

    6. Accept change

        The change will need to be signed off just as requirements are signed off and for the same reasons as covered in ISEB Syllabus Section 9.

        The people who sign it off must have the recognised authority to do so.

    7. Schedule change.

        The change may go in to the current project, or a phase within the project, or a subsequent project and so on. When will it be implemented?

    8. Implement change.

        Doing the work to implement the change to all the areas that need to be changed.

    Note: at any point in the process the change may be rejected

Questions? ISEBRE@smart-BA.com

3. **Traceability and ownership of requirements**

In order to manage changes to requirements at any point in the Systems Development Life-Cycle (SDLC) there must be full backwards and forwards traceability of the requirement:

- Who was involved in generating the requirement?
- When was the requirement generated?
- Who signed it off as a requirement?
- When was it signed off?
- What objectives does it contribute to achieving?
- What processes does it impact?
- What data areas does it impact?
- What non-functional requirements does it impact?
- What modules implement it?
- What databases implement it?
- What screens are impacted?
- What reports are impacted?
- What other functionality is impacted?
- What tests prove its delivery?
- What migration and cutover activities will be impacted?
- What areas of the business will be impacted (organisation and location)?

The methods of recording this vary by organisation – one method is CASE and CARE tools (see below).

The main issue here is to understand why it is important to have the backwards and forwards traceability for requirements: so that full and thorough impact assessments can be made in the event of change and to be able to justify why every element of the solution is required, who requested it and why.

Questions? ISEBRE@smart-BA.com

4. CASE (Computer Aided Software Engineering) tools for Requirements Engineering

- They are a centralised repository of requirements that are used by many groups:

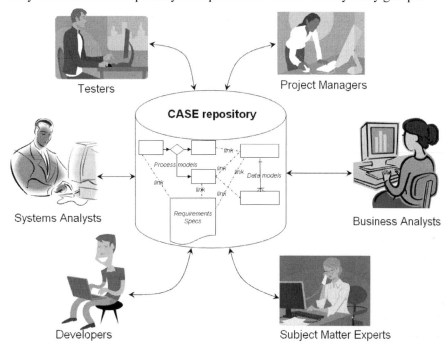

- There are CARE (Computer Aided Requirements Engineering) tools but these are being merged with CASE

    Essentially the same as CASE, CARE just focuses on documenting and managing requirements. The two sets of tools seem to be merging.

- The advantages are concerned with re-use and impact analysis benefits.

    Reuse: A Business Analysis creates a requirement in the CASE tool which can be picked up by a Subject Matter Expert and validated, used by a Systems Analyst to design a solution, Developers to check what they should be coding, Testers to write test scripts, and Project Managers to review progress.

    Impact Analysis: because all of the elements in analysis link together (objectives link to requirements which in turn link to process and data models and associated non-functional requirements), a CASE tool can report on (for a given requirement that a change is proposed for) what objectives are affected, what process models, what data those process models use, where that data in turn gets used by process models and so on.

    CASE tools can also do some *limited* rules based checking to validate the quality of the analysis.

- The disadvantages are cost and how incorrect use makes a big mess very quickly!

    CASE tools are not cheap and, like any tool, if anyone uses it without understanding what they are doing then the information can become wrong very quickly and then be reused by lots of different individuals and groups.

Questions? ISEBRE@smart-BA.com

Further Reading for Syllabus Section 10

Business Analysis – Debra Paul and Donald Yeates
Published by: The British Computer Society
ISBN 1-902505-70-0
Price: £20.00 from BCS and Amazon etc
Relevant Chapters/sections:
  Chapter 9 section Managing Changes to Requirements Pages 156-157

Requirements Engineering by Gerald Kotonya and Ian Sommerville
Published by: John Willey & Sons
ISBN: 0-471-97208-8
Price: £36.00 from Amazon etc
Relevant Chapters/sections:
  Chapter 5 section 5.1 Stable and volatile Requirements pages 115-117
  Chapter 5 section 5.3 Change Management pages 123-134

Writing Better Requirements by Ian F Alexander and Richard Stevens
Published by Addison-Wesley
ISBN 0-321-13163-0
Price £27.50 from Amazon etc
Relevant Chapters/sections:
  Chapter 6 section 6.5 Keeping track of the Requirements pages 92-95

Questions? ISEBRE@smart-BA.com

ISEB Syllabus Section 10 exam style revision question

Close to implementation a change is requested to the following requirements: The system must default the delivery address for a new order to the customer billing address that came from Mr A Smith.

Describe how you would assess the impact of a change to the requirement in terms of who you would see and what you would ask them about.

Stakeholder	Subjects to be discussed	Role

If you want a review of your answers by a Business Analyst please complete the question and email your answer to ISEBRE@smart-BA.com. There is a charge for this service - please pay online at http://www.smart-ba.com/purchase

ISEB Syllabus Section 10 exam style revision question MODEL ANSWER

Stakeholder	Subjects to be discussed	Role
Mr A Smith	Confirm change to requirement What objectives does it contribute to achieving? What tests prove its delivery? What areas of the business will be impacted (organisation and location)?	Sponsor
Ms D Bartlett	What migration and cutover activities will be impacted?	Project Manager
Ms C Gray	What areas of the business will be impacted (organisation and location)? What tests prove its delivery? What processes does it impact? What data areas does it impact? What non-functional requirements does it impact? What reports are impacted? What other functionality is impacted?	Domain Expert
Mr E Clarke	What processes does it impact? What data areas does it impact? What non-functional requirements does it impact? What reports are impacted? What other functionality is impacted?	End user
Mr B Jones	What modules implement it? What databases implement it? What screens are impacted?	IT Domain Expert

Notes:
1. There are no hard and fast rules here and so long as your suggestions are reasonable.
2. Notice that the Sponsor is engaged to confirm the requirement and clarify the objective(s) it contributes to.

©Guy Beauchamp 2009

Questions? ISEBRE@smart-BA.com

smart·BA
distance learning programme

ISEB Syllabus Section 11: Benefits Confirmation

Key points:

1. Requirements testing/User Acceptance Testing (UAT)
   a. Requirements testing proves that the requirement is available in the new system – therefore requirements need to be testable.
   b. User Acceptance Testing is the execution of tests that the users have agreed will (if passed) mean the solution is acceptable.
   c. UAT will be based on requirements as requirements are what the users need in the system in order to achieve the objectives and realise the benefits of the change.

2. Post-implementation Review
   a. Business benefits will not be realised until the solution has been implemented. Therefore, it is not until post-implementation that the delivery of benefits can be monitored.
   b. The review can also analyse other components of the projects such as what went well and what did not (lessons learnt)
   c. In theory a project should not close down until the review has occurred since the declaration of project success (or otherwise) cannot be made until benefits realisation has been monitored and that cannot be done until post implementation.

3. Roles of requirements actors
   a. Accountability for the delivery of project lies with the Project Manager.
   b. The success of the project is defined by the how well the benefits are realised.
   c. Therefore accountability for benefits realisation lies with the Project Manager.
   d. The Business Analyst can tell the Project Manager how to monitor benefits (these will after all have been specified in requirements).
   e. The Business Analyst can also tell the Project Manager what the objectives were.
   f. The Project Manager should report on benefits realisation to the Sponsor and other stakeholders who made the formal decisions to allow the project to progress.

Questions? ISEBRE@smart-BA.com

smart·BA
distance learning programme

Detail

1. **Requirements testing/User Acceptance Testing (UAT)**

   a. Requirements testing proves that the requirement is available in the new system – therefore requirements need to be testable.

   We considered this in ISEB Syllabus Section 7 and 8.2. If the requirement cannot be tested it can never be proved that it has been delivered.

   In order to be able to prove that it has not only been delivered, but that it has been accepted by the users as delivered, a series of targets must be defined that – once achieved – mean that the users have accepted the requirement as delivered.

   For example, consider the requirement that the address postcode must be validated as existing. What tests do the users want to run to prove to their satisfaction that the requirement has been delivered?

   - every postcode is to be run through the process to see if the solution picks it up?
   - Every non-postcode combination of 8 characters is run through to check that it isn't?
   - Etc etc etc!!!

   The point is that usually there are an infinite number of tests that **could** be run but this is impractical, so what subset of these tests are **needed** in order to prove to user satisfaction that the requirement is delivered?

   b. User Acceptance Testing is the execution of tests that the users have agreed will (if passed) mean the solution is acceptable. *It is **not** just letting the users "play" on the system and see if they can break it!*

   The easiest and most obvious way to construct these tests is to use the scenario modelling covered in ISEB Syllabus Section 9.1 as the **basis** of the tests

   Consider one of the scenario examples given in that section:

   1. "Customer" orders goods to be delivered to default delivery address.

      1.1. The Solution displays a list of known "Customer" delivery addresses with the default delivery address already selected and prompts the "Telesales Order Team Member" to ask the "Customer" if they want to use their default delivery address.

      1.2 The "Telesales Order Team Member" records that the "Customer" does want to use the default delivery address.

      1.3 The Solution associates the default delivery address with customer order and prompts the "Telesales Order Team Member" to confirm.

      1.4 The "Telesales Order Team Member" confirms.

   The scenario could be used as the start of a test script: the script tells the tester what to do:

No	Action	Expected Response	Result (success or fail and notes)
1	Create an "Order" for a "Customer" using system functionality.	The Solution displays a list of known "Customer" delivery addresses with the default delivery address already selected and prompts the "Telesales Order Team	

No	Action	Expected Response	Result (success or fail and notes)
		Member" to ask the "Customer" if they want to use their default delivery address.	
2	The "Telesales Order Team Member" records that the "Customer" does want to use the default delivery address	The Solution associates the default delivery address with customer order and prompts the "Telesales Order Team Member" to confirm.	
3	The "Telesales Order Team Member" confirms	The system saves the association.	
4	Inspect the order record.	The order delivery address is the default delivery address for the "Customer".	

Further information is needed before the test can be run though: what state does the system need to be in order to be able to start running the test script? Some **data** will need to be in place before the user can run the script. Example:

"USER" A user type "telesales order team member" is required for the person executing the test.

"CUSTOMER" a normal customer.

"PRODUCT" at least one product that can be ordered by the customer is needed.

Test scripts will also be (typically) part of a series so that there will be a test script that was run before this one (in this case to create the default delivery address for the customer) and one that runs after it (in this case perhaps one that allows the user to change the delivery address for the order under certain circumstances).

And finally audit information will be needed to manage the (typically) large number of test scripts that a project will have (such as author, execution date, outcome of test and so on).

c. UAT will be based on requirements as requirements are what the users need in the system in order to achieve the objectives and realise the benefits of the change.

Given that project success is defined by achieving objectives (i.e. benefits) then it is critical to test that these have been achieved. Requirements, remember, are defined as those things which need to change in order for the system to deliver the objectives. Therefore, test the requirements are being delivered and you test that the things that need to change in order to achieve the objectives are being delivered.

Remember as well that requirements are ultimately generated by and signed-off by users. In essence this forms a contract of what will be delivered regardless of how it is delivered. So it makes a lot of sense for the users to check that they agree that what has been agreed to be delivered in terms of requirements actually has been delivered.

Questions? ISEBRE@smart-BA.com

2. **Post-implementation Review (PIR)**

   a. Business benefits will not be realised until the solution has been implemented. Therefore, it is not until post-implementation that the delivery of benefits can be monitored.

   The reality of this is that financial benefits can take years to accumulate so one issue is when to have the PIR. The majority of costs will have been expended during the development – although there will be on-going operational costs as well. While some benefits (such as compliance with legal requirements that enable to business to continue trading) will occur immediately, the same can not be said for (typically) those that involve saving money and making money. This can lead to a significant gap between implementation and PIR, or no PIR of benefits, or a strategy of continuous monitoring of delivery (something that methods such as Six Sigma have a major emphasis on). Whichever approach is adopted, logic dictates this should have been debated and agreed during the project initiation. In any event, the fact the project deliverables have been delivered can and should be recorded.

   b. The review can also analyse other components of the projects such as what went well and what did not (lessons learnt).

   Lessons learnt should be learnt from all stakeholders engaged on the project. Other elements that could be considered during the review are recommendations for subsequent enhancements (perhaps based on de-scoped requirements), acknowledgement and a plan of action for any outstanding issues, and any general user feedback.

   c. In theory a project should not close down until the review has occurred since the declaration of project success (or otherwise) cannot be made until benefits realisation has been monitored and that cannot be done until post implementation.

   Project success = achieving objectives = benefits realisation.

3. **Roles of requirements actors**

   a. Accountability for the delivery of project lies with the Project Manager.

   b. The success of the project is defined by the how well the benefits are realised.

   c. Therefore accountability for benefits realisation lies with the Project Manager.

   It is worth noting that a lot of project managers are judged on project delivery on time and to budget. The project itself will be judged on benefits realisation. This can be unfortunate as what actions a project manager should take to deliver a project on time and to budget are not always the same actions they should take to realise the benefits of the project deliverables.

   d. The Business Analyst can tell the Project Manager how to monitor benefits (these will after all have been specified in requirements).

   In any project there will (almost) always be management information reports that report on the objectives – because they are the important measures that the business measures its success by and because without them how will a project be able to prove it has been successful?

   e. The Business Analyst can also tell the Project Manager what the objectives were.

   The Project Manager may have documented the Objectives with the Sponsor but then again they may not – or they may have not done it with enough rigour to allow the Business Analyst to map all requirements to the objectives they help deliver. In any event,

Questions? ISEBRE@smart-BA.com

the Business Analyst must have as a starting point a set of objectives that they can use to control the scope of the project by mapping requirements to. It is these objectives (whoever documented them) that the Business Analyst can inform the Project Manager were used to control project scope and are being used to measure project success.

f. The Project Manager should report on benefits realisation to the Sponsor and other stakeholders who made the formal decisions to allow the project to progress.
The Sponsor and other accountable stakeholders need the information to know whether they are getting the benefits they expected.

Questions? ISEBRE@smart-BA.com

ISEB Syllabus Section 11 exam style revision question

For the scenario you modelled in ISEB Syllabus Section 9 exam style question, document a user acceptance test script for just the happy day scenario: The "Customer" has a standard delivery address with no changes required.

Use the following format:

Data set up:

No	Data entity	Set up notes
1		
2		
3		
4		
5		

Test script:

No	Action	Expected Response	Result (success or fail and notes)
1			
2			
3			
4			
5			

If you want a review of your answers by a Business Analyst please complete the question and email your answer to ISEBRE@smart-BA.com. There is a charge for this service - please pay online at http://www.smart-ba.com/purchase

©Guy Beauchamp 2009
Questions? ISEBRE@smart-BA.com

ISEB Syllabus Section 11 exam style revision question MODEL ANSWER

Data set up:

No	Data entity	Set up notes
1	Telesales Order Team Member	Able to log on and create an order
2	Customer	New customer with only 1 order
3	Address	A series of addresses than can be selected

Test script:

No	Action	Expected Response	Result (success or fail and notes)
1	Using the existing functionality, create the first order for the customer.	The solution prompts the "Telesales Order Team Member" to capture the "Customer's" house number or name and postcode.	
2	The "Telesales Order Team Member" enters the "Customer's" house number or name and postcode.	The solution displays the full address and prompts for confirmation.	
3	The "Telesales Order Team Member" confirms the address with the "Customer".	The solution associates the address with the "Customer" as the default delivery address.	

Maximise your marks in the ISEB Requirements Engineering exam

Key points:
1. Exam format – Open book, 15 minutes reading time, 1 hour writing time
2. Reading time – take in this manual! Take in small post-its to mark relevant pages. Plan what order to answer questions
3. Writing time – read each question in your preferred order and then answer the question, the whole question and nothing but the question, and refer all answers to the scenario – the exam is testing your ability to *do* requirements engineering!

Detail:
1. **Exam format – Open book, 15 minutes reading time, 1 hour writing time**
   - The room will be laid out exam style: 1 person per desk, all desks face forward, clock clearly visible.
   - Your exam pack will consist of:
     i. ISEB exam cover sheet
     ii. Exam paper
        - Scenario outlining the context for the analysis you will be asked to do in the exam
        - Around 4 to 8 questions asking you to do requirements engineering on the scenario
     iii. Several sheets of A4 for writing your answers on
   - You will be asked to complete the exam front sheets and you should write your name on all the A4 answer sheets as well.
   - No talking from here on in unless you need help from the invigilator such as more paper.
   - Then you get 15 minutes to read the exam paper.
   - Then you get 1 hour to answer the exam questions.
   - Materials:
     i. You can take any books etc you like in to the exam but not a laptop or mobile phone.
     ii. Take a couple of black ink pens with you (in case one runs out!) and a ruler.
     iii. Take some post it notes so that you can mark relevant pages during the reading time.
     iv. If you have any questions about what is allowed and what is not ask us and/or ask the invigilator on the day.

2. **Reading time – take in this manual! Take in small post-its to mark relevant pages. Plan what order to answer questions.**
   - The reading time is 15 minutes. Read the scenario AND the questions.
   - Reread the scenario.
   - Read the questions again. Note that the breadth of topics covered in Requirements Engineering means that you will not have a question on every topic.

Questions? ISEBRE@smart-BA.com

- For each question think if you need to reference any sections of the books you have brought in with you. **DO NOT WRITE ANYTHING DOWN!** You can use the post-its to mark any passages you think might help but you must not write anything down or even pick up your pen!
- Plan to answer the questions in the following order:
   i. those you are confident you can answer and have high marks
   ii. those you are confident you can answer and have lower marks
   iii. those you are less confident about and have high marks
   iv. those you are less confident about and have lower marks

3. **Writing time – read each question in your preferred order and then answer the question and refer all answers to the scenario – the exam is testing your ability to *do* requirements engineering!**
   - Answer the questions in your planned order.
   - **Read the question** to make sure you understand it. There are countless examples of candidates who have (for example) drawn an excellent process model but have been awarded no marks for it as it was for the wrong process! Some candidates write the essence of the question out as part of the answer and this seems to help them and the examiner.
   - **Answer the question**. There are no marks for elements of analysis that the question does not call for. If you think the question could be interpreted in multiple ways, state how you have interpreted it. If you need to make an assumption to answer the question, state the assumption. The examiners are looking for reasons to give you marks so give them as much evidence as you can that the answer in the context of the scenario, how you have interpreted the question and the assumptions you have made is correct.
   - **Remember to answer the question, the whole question and nothing but the question!** If the exam question asks for 5 of something, do not bother doing more than 5: the examiner will mark the first 5 and ignore the rest. If you do not want an examiner to mark an answer, clearly strike it through. Do not add information that is not asked for by the question or needed to justify your answer: you are wasting time.
   - **The examiners want you to pass**! They cannot just award or take away marks arbitrarily – there is a definite marking process to follow, extensive marking guidelines and random papers are checked by ISEB. So the awarding of marks has to be justified by written evidence of the correct answer to the exam questions. Make sure that you give the examiners as much information as you need to in order to show that you can do the analysis the question asks you to do.
   - *Refer to the scenario*! This is a test of your ability to **do** requirements engineering not quote textbooks – in fact examiners have instructions to mark down answers that do not reference the scenario and explain how – in the context of the scenario – the analysis would be done.
   - Write as neatly as you can – there are no marks for neatness but the markers are human and if they can't easily read your answer they are going to struggle to award you marks!
   - **Name any processes as verb+noun!**
   - Keep an eye on the time – try not to spend more than 10 minutes on any one question.
   - If you have any spare time check your answers. You have to stay for the full hour so you might as well use all of it.

Questions? ISEBRE@smart-BA.com

ISEB Requirements Engineering Sample Exam Paper and Marking Scheme

There is a sample paper and marking scheme from the BCS ISEB website at
http://www.bcs.org/upload/pdf/resample.pdf and http://www.bcs.org/upload/pdf/remark.pdf and is
downloadable from there and also available in the material accompanying this manual…

The following pages are another sample paper that you should attempt to answer and then review the
marking scheme answers that follow it.

*This exam is presented for you to check your ability to take the exam – hence it is in your interests to take
the exam in conditions which closely mimic the actual exam.*

If you want a review of your answers by a Business Analyst please complete the exam paper and email your
answer to ISEBRE@smart-BA.com. There is a charge for this service - please pay online at
http://www.smart-ba.com/purchase

INFORMATION SYSTEMS EXAMINATION BOARD

CERTIFICATE

IN

REQUIREMENTS ENGINEERING

<u>MOCK</u> EXAM PAPER – SBA/RE/001/v1.0

ISEB Certificate in Requirements Engineering
Self Study 'JEEP' Manual

distance learning programme

Time Allowed: 1 hour

You are allowed fifteen (15) minutes reading time before the examination starts. You are not allowed to write anything during that reading time.

This is an open-book examination which means that you can refer to written material in addition to the examination paper itself.

Write in blue or black ink only.

Please write your name at the top of each piece of paper used for your answers.

Attempt ALL questions. All questions are based on the same scenario.

Marks may be deducted for spurious and irrelevant answers.

State any assumptions made.

There are 52 marks in total for this paper. The pass mark is 26.

The mark awarded for each separate question will be shown with the question text.

smart·BA
distance learning programme

Scenario – YourCall

YourCall is a large company offering an outsourcing service to other companies who want call centre capabilities but do not want to operate a call centre. YourCall runs a 'virtual' call centre for these companies by setting up dedicated teams to service each company they take on. YourCall operates two large call centres both in Scotland (Glasgow and Fort William) but the head office is in London.

YourCall measures it's performance by a number of factors, the most important ones being Average Handling Time (AHT) and Call Hand-Offs (CHO) which is where a call is transferred from one advisor to another. They have a "1 and 1" strategic target for the measures meaning 1 minute per call and no more than 1 hand off. All projects must contribute to achieving the strategy.

You have been engaged to model a new process called "conduct internet chat" with customers – the idea is that customers would be on a company website that wants to offer this service and instead of phoning to talk to an advisor they would click on a link to start a web based chat. This would redirect them to the YourCall website chat application known as Chatterbox which would determine if an online advisor is available. All online advisors will be located at the Glasgow call centre in a new organisation unit called "Internet Contact Team" which would be part of the Customer Services Division. If an advisor is available then the source website that the customer came from is passed to the advisor and the advisor and customer start to web chat, with the advisor using their existing systems to handle the web-chat as if it were a telephone call. If there is no available advisor then the customer is notified that they are in a queue and offered phone numbers as an alternative. The customer is held in the queue until an advisor becomes available (and the customer is assigned to that advisor) or the customer abandons the chat request.

The driver behind this change are that YourCall don't want to be left behind as this kind of service is growing in popularity and YourCall want to be seen as innovators. Additionally, there is some evidence to suggest that some customers prefer internet chats as phoning requires more effort than starting an internet chat session and it seems that customers on internet chats order more items per order. The project is being initiated by the Marketing Dept and funded jointly by the Operations and Customer Services Divisions. The Marketing Dept (part of Customer Services Division) also predict savings on the telephony costs as well.

The telephony systems and IT systems are all managed and controlled by the IT Dept who have developed a strategy to ensure reliable provision of services to the call centres.

End of Scenario

ISEB Certificate in Requirements Engineering
Self Study 'JEEP' Manual

smart·BA
distance learning programme

Question 1

Identify the main stakeholders for your work. State why is each stakeholder interested in the project.

8 marks

Question 2

Outline the scope of your piece of work.

5 marks

Question 3a

Suggest 3 possible project objectives.

3 marks

Question 3b

What is your analysis of the fit of this project with the company strategic objectives of "1 and 1"?

2 marks

Question 4

Based on the description of the process "conduct internet chat" what you suggest are the functional requirements?

12 marks

Question 5

Draw a BPMN process model for the process "conduct internet chat". Show
- all start, intermediate and end events
- sequence flows
- gateways
- processes

20 marks

Total Marks Available = 52
Pass Mark = 26

End of Paper

©Guy Beauchamp 2009

Questions? ISEBRE@smart-BA.com

Marking Scheme

Question 1

Identify the main stakeholders for your work. State why is each stakeholder interested in the project.

8 marks

Question 1 - Marking Scheme

1 mark for each valid stakeholder.
1 mark for each valid reason for being involved.

Stakeholder	Interest
Marketing Dept	Initiator.
Customer Services Division	Budget holder.
Operations Division	Budget holder.
IT Dept	Ensure compliance with IT standards.

Question 2

Outline the scope of your piece of work.

5 marks

Question 2 - Marking Scheme

1 mark per valid scope statement (max 5) – examples:
Process: Conduct internet chat
Organisation: Internet Contact Team
Location: Glasgow
Data: Customer, source website, advisor
Application: Chatterbox
Technology: Internet

Question 3a

Suggest up to 3 possible project objectives.

©Guy Beauchamp 2009
Questions? ISEBRE@smart-BA.com

3 marks

Question 3a - Marking Scheme

1 mark per valid objective up to a maximum of 3.
Increase the number of customer enquiries.
Increase the number of items per order.
Maintain compliance with IT strategy.
Maintain 1 minute average call handling time.
Maintain max 1 call hand-offs.
Increase perception of YourCall as innovators.

Question 3b

What is your analysis of the fit of this project with the company strategic objectives of "1 and 1"?

2 marks

Question 3a - Marking Scheme

The company strategic objectives are 1 minute per call and no more than 1 hand off. Internet chats are unlikely to be as swift as calls as the customer is typing. In that sense this project may be non-strategic.

Question 4

Based on the description of the process "conduct internet chat" what you suggest are the functional requirements?

12 marks

Question 4 – Marking Scheme

Up to 2 marks for each functional requirement to a maximum of 12.
Be able to conduct a web based chat between advisor and customer.
Be able to determine if an online advisor is available.
Be able to identify the source website that the customer came from.
Be able to notify customers when they are in a queue for an internet chat.
Be able to assign customer to advisor for internet chat when advisor becomes available.
Be able to offer alternative phone numbers to customers when they are in a queue for an internet chat.

Question 5

Draw a BPMN process model for the process "conduct internet chat". Show
- all start, intermediate and end events
- sequence flows

Questions? ISEBRE@smart-BA.com

- gateways
- processes

20 marks

Question 5 – Marking Scheme

Up to 2 marks for each for
- start, intermediate and end events (to a max 8)
- conditional sequence flows (to a max of 4)
- processes (to a max of 8)
- gateways (to a max of 4)

Note that gateways and conditional process flows can be used interchangeably so the maximum marks available are 20.

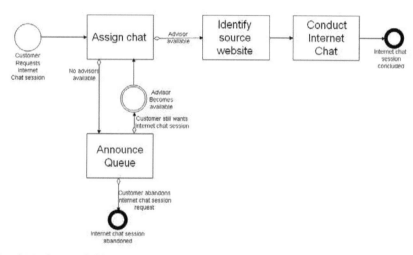

Total Marks Available = 52
Pass Mark = 26

End of Paper

Questions? ISEBRE@smart-BA.com

Review of ISEB Requirements Engineering Objectives

Are you confident you can…

- Describe the roles and responsibilities of key stakeholders in the requirements engineering process
- Demonstrate the application of a range of requirements elicitation techniques
- Explain the use of requirements elicitation techniques and the relevance of the techniques to given situations
- Document and prioritise user requirements for an information system
- Identify problems with requirements and explain how requirements documentation may be improved
- Create a process/function model of requirements for an information system
- Interpret a model of the data requirements for an information system
- Explain the importance of linking project objectives and requirements to the Business Case
- Describe the principles of Requirements Management and explain the importance of managing requirements
- Describe the use of CASE tools to support Requirements Engineering
- Explain the principles of Requirements Validation and define an approach to validating requirements

http://www.bcs.org/server.php?show=nav.7738

If not, go back a revise the sections that you are not confident with or consider taking a course.

If you are, then either contact us to arrange an exam or (of course) arrange your own with any exam provider.

GOOD LUCK!

©Guy Beauchamp 2009
Questions? ISEBRE@smart-BA.com

Glossary of terms

B   Business Requirement – a change (system and/or business) required to deliver *objectives*

C   CARE – Computer Aided Modelling Business Processes

       CASE – Computer Aided Software Engineering

D   Data Requirement – a change to the information required in order to for *processes* or *tasks* to be able to run.

E   External - An external is a person, role, organisation or IT system that is external to the scope of the project (i.e. will not be changed by the project) that the solution the project develops will interact with.

F   Functions are common sub-processes or tasks that

- are used by more than one process
- typically accomplish one significant outcome in terms of either data or directing process flow

       Functional Requirement – a system change required to deliver *objectives*.

G   General Requirement – a requirement that sums up the scope of the project from a requirements perspective

N   Non-functional requirement – a change required to deliver *objectives* that is not a *General, Business, Functional, Data or Technical Requirement*

O   Objectives are measures that can increased, decreased or maintained and if they hit a certain target value equate to project success. For this reason they are the project benefits.

P   PID – Project Initiation Document

       PIR – Post Implementation Review

       Process – a connected series of business activities (at the lowest level these are *tasks*) designed to produce a meaningful outcome for the business

       Process Metrics – measures and target values that define whether the process is running optimally or not.

Q

R   Requirements are defined as those things which need to change in order for the system to deliver the *objectives*.

S   SDLC – Systems Development Life Cycle

T   Task – the lowest level of decomposed *process*

       TOR – Terms of Reference

       Technical Requirement – a constraint imposed on the project in terms of what options are available to design the solution

Questions? ISEBRE@smart-BA.com

YOUR NOTES

Questions? ISEBRE@smart-BA.com

YOUR NOTES

Questions? ISEBRE@smart-BA.com

YOUR NOTES

Questions? ISEBRE@smart-BA.com